Herbert D. Holden

ARTHUR H. STOCKWELL LTD.
Elms Court   Ilfracombe   Devon
Established 1898

ISBN 0 7223 2951-2

Printed in Great Britain by
Arthur H. Stockwell Ltd.
Elms Court   Ilfracombe
Devon

CONTENTS

Chapter 1

Bert and the Gravesend Sea School

Life in any situation, can be funny or it can be sad. Wartime seemed to give a mixture of both. The "comings" and "goings" of its participants were filled with joy and tinged with sadness. Bert's life was to be no exception, starting as a lad still "wet behind the ears" and finishing at the "ripe old age" of twenty-two years, a much-travelled man of the world. He was born and bred in the Port of Liverpool, being the eldest and only son of Lil and Perce Holden. The other two children being Sybil and Muriel. No doubt Perce Holden would admit that their life had been sheltered up to that fateful day in September 1939 when events were to turn the world upside down.

Sunday morning, 3rd September, seemed to be the same as any other Sunday to Bert. He was delivering Sunday papers for a local newsagent. The money earned, helped to swell his five shillings and ten pence per week that he earned as an apprentice motor mechanic, at Blake's garage and showrooms, Safety Lane off Brownlow Hill.

Nearing the end of his round, a customer opened her door and said "We are at war with Germany." Riding home on his bicycle his imagination was running riot. He thought of the past glories of the British Empire and of other great wars that he had been taught, only a few weeks ago, at school. He was proud to be British and was quite sure that in no time at all, Britain would be showing those Germans, led by "Adolf" who was boss.

Arriving home, he was surprised to find his mother in tears. Those very same tears were to haunt him and fill him with guilt, as the war years dragged on and human suffering spread throughout the world. However on that Sunday morning, when great events were about to take place, it would have to be a female to show signs of weakness by crying. Now was the time to be proud and happy;

5

Britain was at last showing she was great. The old lion was finally showing its teeth. Logic was not part of a sixteen-year-old boy's thinking.

The Donaldson liner, *Athenia*, was torpedoed that first day, with heavy loss of life. This further fanned the feeling of patriotism and righteous anger in the British people. Bert was one of many thousands, who at that terrible announcement of the sinking on the wireless, would have killed a German himself. The following week saw the British Expeditionary Force, including Bert's favourite Uncle Bill, a gunner in the Royal Artillery, shipped to France. Then came the lull. The only action seemed to be taking place at sea, with shipping losses mounting steadily. To the "civvies" at home, it became known as the "phoney war".

With the build-up of troops in France, many regiments marched through Liverpool to the Pier Head, where great liners were moored at the landing stage waiting to embark the soldiers. Embarkation of troops was also taking place at the North End Docks. This movement of troops led by army bands, had an unsettling effect on Bert, who unfortunately was going through a period of inactivity caused by a severe case of blood poisoning. A cut at work had turned very nasty and he had been off work for six weeks.

During this period, he became very restless and discontented, until one evening he presented himself to the local Royal Engineer Barracks, to try to enlist as a boy bugler. His father had been a lance corporal with the same unit a few years before, so he imagined his enlistment would be only a formality. All his romantic dreams came tumbling down when he was refused enlistment because of his age. In later years he was to learn how lucky he had been in not being accepted, because most of the unit were either killed or captured in Crete.

Listening to the wireless, shortly afterwards, he could hardly believe his ears. There was an appeal for young boys to be trained as deck boys, at the Gravesend Sea School. They would be required to complete a three months' course and then pass a Proficiency Certificate in General Seamanship, which would enable them to join the British Merchant Navy and sail on any ship that they so wished.

He approached his father for permission to apply, which was grudgingly given. His father had been associated with seamen for over twenty-six years, being the organist for the Gordon Smith Institute for Seamen, playing the organ for their Sunday morning service. His first job on leaving school had been working for a ship repairer, namely Graysons and Rollo. Living in a sea port he had an affinity with the sea and ships. Bert often thought that his father would have liked to be a seafarer and this proved to be true when later in the war his father applied for gun crews in the Merchant Navy.

Bert sent off a letter of application to the school and after what seemed to be eternity, received back, the appropriate forms with a letter informing him that he had been accepted, subject to his passing a doctor's examination. He passed the medical, but only just. The minimum chest measurements were thirty-two inches and he was barely thirty-one and a half. The doctor told him that he would no doubt fill out when he grew older. With his forms and medical report sent back to the school board, he had an agonising wait for word to say that he had been accepted.

As the weeks dragged by he began to despair. He would race to the door when he heard a letter dropping to the floor, only to be disappointed when he saw that it was not for him. Eventually the letter arrived, telling him to report to the TS *Vindicatrix*, moored at the canal berth, Sharpness, Gloucestershire on 18th December 1939. At that moment of time he was over the moon, not knowing what heartaches were before him, even before he "put to sea".

The 18th December eventually came; cold and wet. Bert was not sorry to board the train at Lime Street Station. The worst part was over — the hugs and tears from his mother and sisters. Probably his worst moment was when his father gave him a manly hug and handshake. The emotion between them was electric. As the train pulled out of the station, he felt suddenly proud and grown up. He was actually on his way to doing his share in Britain's war effort. This cushioned the effects of leaving his family for the first time.

Six hours later the train pulled into Sharpness Station where he disembarked, feeling cold, hungry and all alone. The countryside was dark in the winter evening, obliterated by the blackout. Bert thought that it was blacker than the city. He suddenly asked himself "What the hell am I doing here?"

Following instructions from a kindly ticket collector, he groped his way down what he was told, was a country lane. It would have been much easier without his heavy suitcase. At the bend in the lane he had to leave the tar and feel with his feet for a footpath that would take him across one of the locks between the canal and the docks. Having negotiated the lock successfully he had to find the other part of the footpath which was by no mean feat with there being high blackberry bushes on either side. Having found the path once more he walked on with what he presumed were fields on either side, because he could hear cows or horses moving restlessly. Eventually he came to another bridge over what appeared to be the canal. In daytime you could see the ship easily from this point, but at night with no moon you could see nothing, which no doubt was a good thing. Crossing the bridge and walking along the canal bank he became aware of a black hulk in the canal. It was indeed the *Vindicatrix*, kindly almost hidden away by the blackout. Eventually Bert came across a rather steep gangway. Thankfully he climbed it and went aboard.

Once on board, all his romantic dreams slipped away. An officer booked him in and he was shown to his bunk. There was no meal and no cup of tea after his long journey. This then was the harsh realities to the real life. He was at that moment too hungry and tired even to feel homesick. The sleeping deck or dormitory came as a severe shock to him. It was a long deck, with rows and rows of two-tiered bunks, sleeping 350 boys. There was no privacy and although no prude, he did find some of the boys' behaviour, offensive.

Waking next morning, conditions were worse than they had appeared the night before. He was amazed to find the deck head covered with four inch icicles; the results of the boys' breath condensing and then freezing. Jumping out of his bunk he shuddered with the intense cold. It was like waking up inside a giant refrigerator. The ship did not have the luxury of a heating system. In her more illustrious days the *Vindicatrix* had been an iron-hulled sailing ship called the *Arranmore* plying the seas between England and Australia. Now stripped of all her glamour, she seemed determined to break the spirit of all but the most hardened of the boys. The boys themselves, were a motley-looking bunch, with their funny little pointed hats hanging over one ear. They were issued with blue rolled-neck jumpers and navy-coloured jeans. Bert thought that they looked like a young version of a pirate crew. There were boys from Ireland, Scotland and Wales besides English boys. In the bunk under Bert's, there was an Indian boy. It was a real cross section of boys from so many varieties of life — good and bad. One common bond between the boys was, they were British and proud of it. Their school song, to the tune of 'Anchors Aweigh', went as follows:

"We are the Sea School Boys, Britain's pride and joy.
We joined the Merchant Navy, to bring food into our country.
U-boats we'll never fear, we'll sink them all.
Send the U-boats to the bottom, sink the U-boats
Sink the U-boats all."

This song was likely to "burst" out at any time and to be sung with much gusto.

The morning after his arrival was exploring time. That is, exploring his home for the next three months. There was not much to see of any great interest on the various decks, so he decided he would make his way down the gangway and view the ship from the outside. Standing on the canal bank he could see how ugly she was. He could never imagine how sails could possibly drive her before the wind to Australia. She looked like a huge iron box. Her top deck consisted of sheds painted grey. He was to learn later that these sheds were to house 350 boys having their body "wash downs". Walking along the canal about 220 yards from the ship were the toilets. The building could have been an old stable backing onto the River Severn. Two great drains ran its length and out under the back wall, carrying its contents into the river. A rough seating arrangement allowed the boys to sit over the open drains, without them falling into the drain. Unfortunately the endless icy blast of a severe winter, deterred all but the desperate. To arrive back from a night-time visit, was like re-boarding the *Queen Mary* and all her luxury.

As the days passed by and Bert settled into the Spartan routine, his appetite grew as did the appetite of the other 349 boys. The exercise, mostly open air and the very small meals, made for hungry stomachs. At every meal food changed hands for a price. Slices of bread, pieces of greasy boiled pudding and slices of cheese were regularly sold across the table, to eager buyers who had spare cash. However the main meal was always eaten, no matter how unappetising. This was needed for filling, the same as the porridge at breakfast time. Every day, a lifeboat would be rowed along the canal, through the locks into the docks, to pick up the bread supply for the school. Four tea chests would be filled at the bakery, with double tinned loaves. It was never necessary to ask for volunteers to man the lifeboat. The boys not in class would stay round the boat until the officer appeared and then there would be a mad scramble to jump into the boat.

On arrival at the pick-up point, the boys would swiftly remove one double loaf, while the officer was arranging for the other chests to be filled. In a matter of seconds the hungry boys had devoured the double loaf. It was seldom that Bert missed one of these trips and became an expert at making loaves disappear. He was also very fortunate to have a family who could afford to send him food parcels. This helped to make life more tolerable for him.

Inside the ship were great scuppers through which the wind would blow. These were relics of the days when giant seas would wash overboard and were necessary to allow the water to run back into the sea. Classes from week one to eleven were held in the mess deck. The boys could not say that the lessons were very taxing, in fact Bert found them to be quite easy. Study in one's spare time made it easy to keep up with the course.

Having quite a lot of spare time meant that young boys would get themselves into trouble. Bert was no exception and in doing so received a very valuable lesson in life (fortunately without cost, except maybe to his ego). A few boys in the senior classes, were appointed 'boatswains mates', much the same as other schools appoint 'prefects'.

One particular 'free' morning Bert was throwing stones across the canal into a group of steel barges. Along came a boatswains mate and told him to "Cut it out". A few boys from Bert's class happened to be nearby, so Bert in a cheeky voice said "Make me". The other boy told him that he did not want any trouble, to which he received raucous laughter from all the boys. Thinking to himself that he had made himself a big man, Bert was disillusioned on the Friday night when grudges were settled in the "ring" supervised by an officer. This very same boatswains mate entered the ring with the school bully who was a giant of a lad. Imagine everyone's surprise when the boatswains mate gave the big fellow a boxing lesson. With every blow that landed and there were so many Bert kept whincing and thinking that could have been me. The boatswains mate was an amateur boxer and must have known that he could have taken him with one hand and blindfold. It was a priceless lesson and one that he found most useful when he left the school.

As mentioned earlier, the wash sheds were on top deck. Every Friday the boys would form a single line and wait their turn to enter one of these sheds. The sheds had no doors and standing naked with the wind howling across the River Severn was something beyond expression. Each lad entering a shed would be handed a piece of scrubbing soap and a bucket of hot water. When all the boys in the shed had covered themselves with a lather an officer would turn a hose of cold water onto them, to wash off the soap. They would file out of another door into a dressing room to dress with clean clothes. Once dressed they had the task of "dhobiing" (washing their clothes). The boys would feel as if their skin was on fire for quite a considerable time after their ablutions. Bert thought about his mother who brought them up to believe that cleanliness was next to godliness. He wondered how that was possible because after such an ordeal he did not feel very godlike.

Christmas had been a very drab occasion on board the *Vindicatrix*. There was no special fare and most boys were feeling very homesick, none more so than those like Bert who were just starting on their course. The weather had become increasingly cold and huge ice floes were floating down the River Severn. Bert slipped into the canal up to his waist and before he could walk the twenty feet to the gangway his jeans were frozen stiff.

In his third week he met two other boys who were planning to leave the school without telling the captain. Bert became interested in their plan and decided to join them. He could not bring himself to write for his return fare home, so with the other two boys, decided to hitchhike. There was a rail bridge across the river so they decided to cross on this. The following Sunday after lunch, when everything was quiet, was chosen as the best time.

Sunday afternoon came and the three boys carrying their cases slipped quietly down the gangway. Bert facing a one-hundred miles walk and one of the other boys an even longer trip to Northern Ireland. They had barely covered one quarter of a mile, when a group of boys caught up with them and told them that they had been sent to take them back by the captain who had seen their departure. Returning to the ship, they were crestfallen on being confronted by the captain (Captain Duguid). He said that they were very silly and if they wanted to return home so badly he would write out a travel warrant for them to do so. The boys agreed to stay, but only Bert kept his promise. The other two boys walked out a week later. Bert stayed on to pass his Proficiency Certificate in nine weeks instead of the usual twelve weeks.

It was during his time at the school that the reality of war and its consequences came home to him. Sharpness was hardly a village let alone a port, consequently there was very little entertainment for the boys except at a cinema two miles away at a place called Berkely Vale. However the docks were quite large and ocean-going freighters were always coming and going. The boys frequented the tiny seamen's mission where they could obtain very good drinking chocolate and play darts. As they walked to the mission they would "eye" the various ships and sometimes would be invited on board. One such ship flying the Greek flag and called the *Ellini Stathos* docked, watched by the boys. In no time they had made friends and were invited on board. The crew of varying nationalities had terrible living conditions and left Bert with a horrible feeling of dread of what was before him in the way of accommodation.

During the four days that the ship was in port they became friends of the crew who were always ready for a chat. Eventually she sailed, with the boys that were able to, waving goodbye to the crew.

Four days later one of the boys passed around a newspaper that he had just purchased and they were all stunned to read "Greek ship, the *Ellini Stathos* torpedoed off Southern Ireland. Eleven men rescued, thirty-three frozen to death in a lifeboat." This first encounter with a doomed ship and the death of men that they had laughed and joked with but a few days before, had a sombre effect on the boys. One that Bert was never to forget, in spite of witnessing many sinkings himself.

In spite of the depression caused by the sinking of the *Ellini Stathos*, the boys were still anxious to complete the course and be off to sea. Bert had received word from home, that he had secured a berth with the Blue Star Line and subject to his passing out from the school was to join the freighter *Sultan Star* when she arrived in Liverpool from Australia. The procedure for passing the Proficiency Certificate was to spend all the eleventh week studying all aspects of sailing a lifeboat and being able to "box the compass". Then in the twelfth week the boys would be seen by Captain Duguid who would give them an individual test in his cabin. Once the test was passed, there was nothing to keep the boys at the school except the issue of the certificate, which was usually the next day.

Bert decided in his ninth week that he would "pick" the brains of the boys already waiting to take the test. Each night he would join the boys waiting outside the captain's door asking relevant questions to the subject until he felt that there was nothing to lose by joining the queue himself. When it was his turn to enter the cabin he felt very philosophic about his chances. So what if he did fail, he was three weeks ahead of his classmates. He could never remember the captain's exact words telling him that he had passed, because he left the cabin in a dream.

The next day was a Friday and he was handed his certificate, together with a rail ticket. This was a day of sheer joy. No matter what lay ahead he was going home and the prospects of his mother's cooking made his mouth water. The boys in his class said he was a lucky dog, but secretly he did not think that luck had entered into it. He had given up a lot of free time when the others were either reading, sleeping or generally "mucking around".

Chapter 2

The *Wellington Star*

Bert's arrival home was that of a hero. Neighbours were waiting to greet him and it made for a very slow walk down his road where his family would be waiting. Finally the great moment arrived when he was nearly swept off his feet by a loving mother and two proud sisters. His father who had helped to carry his suitcase from the station just stood back and laughed.

Later, as things settled down, the joy of his homecoming was tempered by the news given to him by his father, that his "promised" ship the *Sultan Star*, had been torpedoed in the Atlantic on her way home to Liverpool; one seaman having been lost. Bert had long since become aware that this was no game he was about to take part in.

A few days after arriving home from the sea school, he received news from the Blue Star Line that he was to join the *Wellington Star* on 2nd March in the Gladstone Dock. She was the latest refrigerator passenger ship of 11,400 tons in the Blue Star fleet, having just completed her maiden voyage to New Zealand and back. How lucky was he to be offered a deck boy's (or among the seamen, 'Peggy') job on such a wonderful ship. Her top speed was said to be twenty-three knots and she needed that speed because she sailed alone, not in slow convoys.

On 2nd March, his father accompanied him to the Dingle Overhead Railway Station and with much protesting from Bert was persuaded from going no further. He did not want to be seen arriving with his dad in case members of the crew saw him and branded him a baby. Walking away from his father down the dimly-lit ramp, he felt as if he had swallowed a brick. This experience would be repeated many times in the years to come. It never seemed to get any easier, leaving one's loved ones for "parts" unknown.

13

The "Overhead" had always been a ride of mystery to him, since childhood. To look down on the foreign ships with strange names and flags, always fired his imagination. Then there were always fat ugly British tramp steamers, sleek fast freighters, small coasters and giant ocean liners. The six-mile trip to Seaforth was always packed with interest, when you sat on the river side of the carriage.

This morning it was a more subdued boy that travelled this same route. As he looked out of the carriage window he could not help but wonder, what lay before him? He also thought of the men on the *Ellini Stathos*. Had they thought the same as he did now, on their last departure from their loved ones? It was so easy to sing with gusto, the sea school song, "We are the sea school boys" when there were dozens of them around you. Another question uppermost in his mind was, would he measure up and what would he do in a crisis? There would be no father to advise him now.

He alighted from the train at Gladstone Dock Station and "staggered" down the station steps with his kitbag under his arm. He was not strong enough yet to walk with it on his shoulder like the older men. Walking past the policeman on gate duty he entered the dock and there she lay . . . . what a beauty. His misgivings gave way to pride. This was his ship and all the miserable weeks at the sea school now seemed worthwhile. Walking up the gangway, trying to look unconcerned with the heavy weight of his kitbag, he was met by a seaman, who took him to the Purser's Office, to "sign on". This formality completed, he was taken aft to the deck crews' quarters and shown his cabin. It was a pleasant surprise, after what he had seen on board the *Ellini Stathos*. There were two bunks (one above the other) two lockers and a writing table with two chairs. A large mirror was fastened to one bulkhead completing a very functional airy cabin. He was introduced to a twenty-three-year-old, ordinary seaman from Southern Ireland and in spite of the age difference became good seaboard friends. The OS became Bert's protector, especially from a particular AB from Liverpool who liked to bully young boys.

It came as quite a shock to Bert to find the ship moving so soon after signing on. In fact one of the crew almost missed the ship and had to climb aboard in the locks. Their departure must have been brought forward because he had been advised that they would be leaving on the afternoon tide. Leaving Gladstone Dock, he was just a passenger, because everyone was too busy to take notice of him.

Once in the River Mersey and the crew settled down to watch-keeping, he was taken under the wing of the bosun who gave him instructions as regard to his seaboard job. He was to look after the seamen, fetching their meals from the galley which was midships —

quite a feat in rough seas. Clean their washroom, toilets and bathrooms (three). He was to keep them supplied with tea and coffee, making fresh for the various watches throughout the day, besides the day workers. In another mess he had to look after the bosun, lamptrimmer and carpenter. Their quarters were over the seamen's quarters on the poop deck. He was soon to find that these three men, the equivalent of POs in the Royal Navy were indeed gentlemen. It was a pleasure to look after them and found them to be patient and undemanding, completely unlike the seamen, whom he found to be like spoilt children — abusive and unreasonable.

Once a day he had to collect the seamen's rations from the Belgian second steward. No doubt a housewife would have agreed that there was more than ample to feed the men. Bert very carefully divided out the tea, coffee, sugar, tinned milk, butter, bread and jam. His working day started before 7 a.m. and went on until after 8 p.m., consequently he was able to watch the rations. However after he "turned in" the men seemed to have an open go. Next morning there would be nothing left to start the day and then would come the torrent of abuse. In the mess was an electric urn which he kept filled and boiling during the daytime. During the night it would be allowed to run dry and the element would burn out. Time and time again he would have to approach the electrician and very humbly ask that the urn would be repaired. The electrician was fortunately a decent sort of bloke and would repair it immediately. He eventually told Bert that they were a crowd of bloody morons without a brain in their head.

Bert quickly came to the conclusion that deck boys were called 'Peggys' because they could expect to be kicked around like some of the seamen's wives. Evidently, Peggys were there for them to give vent to their feelings during their time at sea.

One morning he was caught making a pot of coffee from the hot-water tap in his bathroom. The water in the *Wellington Star*'s hot-water taps was always near boiling point. During the night the urn had been allowed to run dry and there was the usual heavy griping at Bert. It was then that he decided even if he poisoned some of them he would give them what they wanted via the bathroom. Unfortunately one of the seamen had seen him take the pot into his bathroom. There were howls of rage and threats of a watery grave, but at least it was a diversion and he was told to get the so-and-so urn "fixed" right away.

His biggest fright came however, when he heard a sailor telling his mates in the mess, about one Peggy on a previous ship, being caught putting soda in the teapot. The listeners wanted to know the reason for that, and was told, "To make the tea look strong". Bert with ears pricked thought 'What a great idea'.

The next afternoon at smoko time, he made the usual very large pot of tea (the same pot that always brought about complaints that it was not strong enough). This afternoon he felt very smug, no one had seen him lace the pot with a heap of washing soda. He thought from now on there will be no complaints about the tea's strength. The first two or three seamen entered the mess and after a little time Bert heard "What the bloody hell is this?" followed by other obscenities that made their point. He decided to evacuate his cabin which was next to the mess room but was caught and hauled back by the ear to the mess room. With his head almost pushed inside of the pot, he was asked "What is that?" He looked in horror at the effects of the soda on the pot. The pot that had been heavily coated with tanning, was now shining brightly on the inside and the tea contents had brown skin floating on its surface. One of the seamen's mugs was standing on the table with a terrible-looking liquid filling it. For one terrible moment Bert thought that they might force him to drink it. However they seemed too angry to think of the obvious and seemed content to threaten him. A few with a sense of humour saw the funny side of things which further aggravated those that were not amused. Bert's own admiration for sailors had rapidly diminished and he wished he were big enough to stand up to them. The cook, baker and butcher were his friends and always made him welcome in the galley. It was great going in to pick up the meals, because he was always sure of a laugh.

As a deck boy, Bert received the princely sum of three pounds fifteen shillings per month. He felt that the biggest insult to boys was the danger money allowance. An adult received five pounds per month, a boy only two pounds ten shillings. It did not seem fair, when everyone was in the "same boat" so to speak. Their passage south across the equator was most monotonous. The only interest to Bert was the sighting of Cape Verde Islands, flying fish, whales and albatross. The albatross were fascinating, wheeling and gliding for hours in the wake of the ship. Passing far to the south of the Cape of Good Hope, they turned to sail east across the Indian Ocean. The sheer boredom of the trip was hell to Bert. Four full weeks on board ship for the first trip was something he could never have imagined. At the end of each day there was only his bunk and the weekends were the worst when his mind would wander to what had been happy days when he was free to travel anywhere he wanted on his bicycle with Stewart. If only he had the comfort of a wireless or a gramophone. The nearest the seamen came to music was an AB who had a set of bagpipes. The seamen threatened to throw him and the pipes overboard if he did not stop making such horrible noises. He would then adjourn to the toilet, lock himself in, and proceed making terrible sounds. Another more musical sound was that of a seaman who could not resist singing 'Somewhere over the Rainbow'. He sang this song outward bound and then homeward bound without becoming tired of the tune which was more than could be said for his fellow seamen.

The *Wellington Star* finally arrived in Fremantle on 1st April 1940. The joy of being able to walk along a street again, taking in all the everyday sights that a city dweller takes for granted, was joy sublime to Bert. He gazed with utter enjoyment at the tramcars passing by. Mingling with the busy crowds in the city streets, he felt that once again he was living. Nothing could spoil this wonderful day of once again walking on dry land, after just looking at the restless sea for four whole weeks. The people of Fremantle and Perth did not fail him either. Wherever he went, there were smiles and pleasantries, none more so, than at the Fremantle Flying Angel Seamen's Club. A board of welcome was placed in the mess room, placed in there by the padre of the club, reading "Roll up you Wellington Stars". These clubs situated in every port round the Australian coast were fantastic. The people that were in charge of the running of them, together with the young ladies of the Lighthouse Guild, who were the hostesses to the seamen, made a sailor's time ashore so very pleasant. Every day there was some form of entertainment provided for the seamen with a dance every night and a lovely meal. Before closing, the club would hold a short church service remembering those at sea, led by the club padre. This then was Bert's entertainment round the coast to Sydney and he enjoyed every minute of it.

From Fremantle they had a very rough crossing of the Great Australian Bight on their way to Port Adelaide. Adelaide he found to be a very beautiful city, full of churches and gardens.

Then it was on to Melbourne. Melbourne's wide streets fascinated him, also the number of small cafés and milk bars that served up the most delicious salads with steak. The food was so cheap in those early war years.

The Mecca of the trip as far as he was concerned was Sydney. This was the one city that had interested him more than any other during his school days. It was here that his father's family lived and he longed to meet them. His grandfather had left Liverpool two years or more before he was born and his grandmother, uncles and one aunt had left when he was only six months old. The ship sailed under the great harbour bridge that seemed to dwarf the ship and finally tugs took her in tow and gently pushed and pulled her into her berth at Glebe Island.

Bert had received quite a shock when he entered the mess room. It looked a disaster area, with bottles, cups and a few glasses strewn all over the tables and on the deck. The off-duty seamen had had a binge. To much abuse Bert was told to get the mess cleaned up, because the same men who had caused the mess wanted to know how they were going to sit down for breakfast. He was actually cleaning up when the gangway was lowered and the stevedores started trooping on board. Carrying empty bottles to the deck head, he bumped into a well-dressed man who asked him "Do you know a Bert Holden?" On being told that he was speaking to him, he introduced himself as Uncle Cec. Bert was very embarrassed in meeting this way and just hoped that his uncle did not think that they were his bottles. It was arranged that at the end of the day his uncle would return and take him out to the family home at Granville. He was invited for as many days that he could get leave. Bert had never spoken to the captain and looked on him as some sort of a god. However the desire to spend a few days with his grandparents helped him to overcome the fear of approaching the captain. With shaking legs he knocked on the captain's door and was told to enter. Stating his request in a very halting manner he was surprised when he was given two days off and told that for the rest of time in port he could sleep ashore. As a parting shot, the captain warned him not to be late for duty. His uncle returned as promised and then commenced a most enjoyable tram and train journey to Granville. It was particularly enjoyable to be with someone who knew where he was going, not like when he was alone in the other cities.

The reunion was great and he was made to feel that he was "home". His grandfather, whom he had never seen, was so close to him. It was as if there was a bond between them. Visiting the Blue Mountains, a journey of some seventy-five miles from Granville and then a tour of Sydney, the time passed all too quickly. He spent a few more nights at Granville after work becoming a well-accepted member of the family. His grandfather journeyed with him every morning to his ship and the two never stopped talking. His grandfather did his best to talk him into "jumping ship" and

staying in Australia, but he knew the pull of his own family in England would be too strong.

The morning came for the *Wellington Star* to leave for Newcastle and Brisbane. Much to Bert's joy, he found out that the *Wellington Star* would be once again in Sydney, homeward bound, for about seven days. Her degaussing gear had been severed crossing the Australian Bight. This equipment was vital to protect her against magnetic mines when she arrived back in home waters. The degaussing cable was to be enclosed in a case round the entire perimeter of the hull, hopefully to protect it from heavy seas. It had originally been fitted, held in position by brackets round the hull, but heavy seas had allowed it to break loose and rub on the bows, which cut through the cables like a knife.

Leaving Sydney and sailing north, they encountered a heavy swell, not unusual to this coast. Bert felt ashamed when he became seasick. He had now considered himself a fully-fledged seafarer, long since with his sea legs. Strangely enough he had not been seasick leaving England, but fortunately it was only a five-hour trip to Newcastle.

The ship only spent a few hours in Newcastle discharging the small amount of cargo destined for the port, then they were off on the last leg of their outward bound journey.

Twenty-four hours later they were tied alongside the Queensland Meat Works wharf. The remaining cargo was quickly discharged and then the *Wellington Star* started taking on her frozen cargo of frozen meat and fruit.

The city was fantastic and the weather in late April beautiful. It was great to visit an open-air cinema and sit enjoying it under the stars. The proudest moment of the trip came when the *Wellington Star*'s crew together with the Blue Funnel Line ship *Nestor* (also from Liverpool) were invited to join the Australian armed forces marching through the streets of Brisbane on Anzac Day which was the 25th April. Never before had an unmilitary body of men been so honoured. The march took them along city streets crowded with people. In fact Bert thought that the whole population of Brisbane had turned out.

A church service was held at the Cenotaph and all the local dignatories placed wreathes at the Cenotaph. When they disbanded, the two ships' crews were invited to the Brisbane Flying Angel Seamen's Mission where they were given a great day until closing time. It was a day that he would never forget.

Arriving back in Sydney, he witnessed an incident that he was to enjoy for many a long day. It concerned the AB mentioned earlier in the story as a bully. The ship was alongside the wharf at Pyrmont taking on more frozen cargo. Australian workers were working on the casing for the degaussing gear. The *Wellington Star*'s crew were over the side painting the hull. Nearing the stern, the seamen sent the bully to Bert, with instructions that on no account was he to let anyone use the toilets. The ship had a cruiser stern and consequently any water, or such, would run out over the men working under it. The AB threatened him with drastic action if he did allow the toilets to be flushed. Ten minutes later, this same AB came back over the ship's rail, onto the deck, covered from head to foot with excrement. He was almost breathing fire and threatening to "do" that bastard of a Peggy. Although Bert was completely innocent, he could not account for this incident and was even more puzzled as to the culprit. His threats to kill Bert did not go unnoticed by the young Irishman, who enjoyed every minute of the AB's discomfort. His uncontrolled laughter made the bully remove himself quickly to the bathroom. Turning to Bert, the Irishman said, "You might not have been responsible but honestly it could not have happened to a better bloke. Don't worry he will not lay a finger on you, I will make sure of that."

Eventually the time came to farewell Sydney. It was a hard wrench to leave his new-found family. His grandfather who he was not to see again was visibly upset. Bert had fond memories of him standing alongside the *Wellington Star* patting the side and saying "You have a very fine ship here son." Later events were taken very badly by him and he blamed himself for allowing Bert to leave.

Hobart was the next port of call and they lay alongside the I.X.L. Cannery, taking on board fresh apples and tinned fruit from the cannery. Loading was carried out all too quickly because Hobart was no exception and like the mainland ports they were given a lot of hospitality. Bert became friendly with an old stevedore and would give him tea, jam and bread. When it came time to sail, he appeared with a fresh pineapple for Bert and handed it to him with tears in his eyes. Quite a lot of Hobart's population saw them off, with it being a Sunday afternoon.

Bert suddenly realised it was getting harder to leave the various ports and newly-made friends. However as he was aware all good things must come to an end and the *Wellington Star* cleared Australian waters in the middle of May after six glorious weeks round the coast. As the land receded he began to think of his own home with a certain amount of excitement, but he also realised there was quite a lot of danger to sail through first.

Two weeks of sailing brought them into Table Bay, Cape Town. As they sailed in on that Wednesday morning, there was a sight that they had never seen before. Giant liners like the *Empress of Britain, Empress of Scotland,* the *Andes* and many more, laying at anchor crammed with Australian and New Zealand troops. The

Wellington Star was to have berthed immediately to fill up her fuel tanks, but unfortunately it was to be Saturday morning before she could obtain a berth, owing to the requirements of the liners. As the troopships sailed out heading for the Middle East, they made an impressive sight, with cheering troops crowding their decks and away up into the rigging.

There was drama as the *Wellington Star* was berthing. One of the electric winches hauling in a huge manilla, jammed. As it tightened it started to creak and vibrate under the terrific strain. Bert was about to walk out onto the deck and was warned back by many voices screaming at him to go inside. The electrician who had been summoned, very coolly opened the control panel and pulled the relay, which cut off the power. Had the manilla snapped, it could have seriously injured or decapitated some unfortunate person who happened to be in its path.

There was no shore leave because they were to leave the port in four hours. This was a big disappointment to the crew and left Bert feeling cheated. To think that after two weeks at sea, and then a further three days looking at the land, they could not go ashore. He had so much looked forward to visiting Cape Town and even travelling to the summit of Table Mountain. His grandfather, during his stay in Sydney, had told him tales of the Boer War in which he served with the 16th Lancers. The only consolation now was, they would be home sooner.

It was unfortunate indeed, that they had met up with the troop convoy in Cape Town. They were not able to take on board the required amount of oil, so they were given Las Palmas in the Canary Isles as their new destination to fill up their tanks.

Arriving at the Canary Islands, they were amused to find a French cruiser patrolling outside territorial waters and seven German freighters inside the port flying their swastikas like trapped rats in a trap. Bert felt very proud — at least they could sail freely in and out of ports.

During the refuelling, the crew were able to do a bit of bartering with the locals who came out to them in "bum-boats". Nearly every member of the crew hoisted on board at least one canary. Bert purchased two birds by swapping a large tin of jam for them, making sure none of the crew were around as he did the transaction. The birds came aboard whistling their heads off, but in less than one hour there was not a tweet from any of the birds. A knowing member of the crew explained that when they were being brought out to the ship for barter, their former owners would drop pepper into their throats, causing them to whistle delightfully.

Leaving port later they sailed once again past the seven German ships, feeling nothing but contempt for them. The first real sign of danger appeared next afternoon, when an alert lookout spotted the periscope of a U-boat. Although they were at maximum speed and zigzagging, the captain changed course and they were called to action stations. However she was able to outdistance the U-boat with their superior speed.

Later, Bert was questioned by one of the seamen as to the whereabouts of his sheath knife. No doubt the question had arisen out of the afternoon's close encounter with the U-boat. Admitting that he did not possess one, he was asked "In the eventuality of them having to take to the lifeboats, how would you carry out your small job of cutting free the rope ladder, enabling the crew to climb down it into the boat?" Bert had previously thought about this and replied, "I would climb into the boat, grab the axe and sever the holding ropes with it." How prophetic this answer was to be.

Sunday morning the 16th June, was just another day at sea. The weather was good and the sea calm. They were now entering the Bay of Biscay and in three days time they would be sailing up the River Mersey with a very valuable cargo for the people of the UK. Bert had made a start packing his kitbag with clothes not needed and freshly laundered. He had cleaned his shoes and much to his dismay had found a large block of honey from Australia had melted in the tropics running into one shoe and then setting hard once more. Having scraped and cleaned the honey from the shoe, he was about to pack the shoes away when the *Wellington Star* was shaken violently. His nearest description was, "It was as if a giant had kicked a toy boat". The Irishman was laying on his bunk and quickly realised what had happened. Jumping up he shouted to Bert "We have been hit, get out on deck." As they made for the door the alarm bells began to ring. The *Wellington Star* had a six-inch gun and an anti-aircraft gun on the poop deck. Bert fully expected these to be manned by the two Royal Navy ratings and their own ship's gun crew; however there was nobody near the guns; no doubt because there was no target visible to fire at. He felt completely lost now. Although action stations were still ringing out, what sort of action were they supposed to take? He soon found out when a seaman rushed past him and said "Get to your lifeboat station Peggy." He did as he was told climbing up the ladder to the boat deck. On reaching his boat he was shocked to see the ocean littered with the cargo from the forward hold where the torpedo had hit. There was an increasing trail of carcasses and apples floating out of a gaping hole in number 1 hold. He felt a dreadful sorrow now, because he knew that he was about to lose his "home" of the past three and a half months. In spite of weeks of loneliness and monotony, he had become very attached and proud of the *Wellington Star*. As he stood on the boat deck he felt naked and imagined the U-boat commander looking through his periscope at him.

As the ship's siren sounded abandon ship, other members of the crew appeared on the boat deck. This then was the moment for him to do his little job. Jumping into the lifeboat he grabbed the axe and slashed the rope that held the rope ladder coiled up. As the ladder uncoiled and snaked down towards the water he thought, 'Oh hell, what have I done? Cut the bloody thing right off.' Much to his relief there it was stretched out to the water line from the ship's rail.

The ship's crew lined up at their respective boats and waited the order from the captain to "lower" away. When the order was finally given, Bert together with two seamen, whose job it was to let go of the falls, were lowered in the boat. Finally all four boats were bobbing about in the North Atlantic swell, the crews climbing down the various ladders. Only one man missed stepping into his boat and finished in the water; however willing hands soon hauled him into his boat. Owing to the torpedo hitting for'ard, there had been no casualties, which gave them a lot to be thankful for.

Chapter 3

The Lifeboat

Pulling away from the ship's side it was obvious that the sea was not as smooth as Bert had thought. In fact there was quite a swell and it was not too long before he was "throwing his heart up".

Suddenly a cry went up "There's the bastard." The U-boat broke surface near the four lifeboats. One of the seamen lifted Bert from the bottom of the boat and said, "Look at the U-boat Peggy." Bert however just wanted to be left alone to die. He thought his wish would be answered when the captain of the U-boat steered between the lifeboats. He eventually came out unto the conning tower with a number of seamen carrying a machine gun and rifles. Bert found out later that the U-boat commander was a Captain Frauenheim and he and his crew had sunk a total of 41,500 tons of Allied shipping within a few days (that was including the *Wellington Star*). He appeared to be a gentleman and was concerned about the welfare of the crew. He asked the *Wellington Star*'s captain pertinent questions regarding tonnage, cargo and destination. He apologised for having had to torpedo the ship but said "That is war and it is my duty."

Having made sure that the boats had enough water, he advised the captain to sail due east and if he could make contact with a neutral ship he would tell them we were in the vicinity. Before leaving the boats he gave an order to stay away from the still floating *Wellington Star*, as he intended to put another torpedo into her.

One hour later, the captain decided that the boats pull back to the ship and the crew would reboard her. This was not well received by the crew who could see the awful danger if they were alongside her when the other torpedo hit. Whether the U-boat captain was playing cat and mouse no one was sure, but no sooner had they started rowing towards the ship than there was a great geyser of water followed by a huge explosion and a piece of machinery came out of her funnel. That put paid to that idea. The *Wellington Star* had been torpedoed at 10 a.m. and yet by 2 p.m. she was still riding on the waves as if nothing was wrong with her. What a great ship she was proving to be.

At 2 p.m. the U-boat surfaced again and the gun crew came out on deck and commenced to fire their deck gun at the *Wellington Star*. Thirty-six rounds were fired and thirty-four direct hits were counted.

Bert's seasickness had passed but other members of the crew were becoming sick; it was not a pleasant sight because they had not eaten for a few hours.

As night-time came, the defiant *Wellington Star* was still afloat. She was ablaze from end to end and Bert could not help but think of the poor canaries being roasted alive.

Bert's lifeboat carried sixteen men and himself. The second officer was in charge and on command from the captain in another boat he ordered the hoisting of the sail. With the four boats now under sail, the captain ordered them to sail together. They were 350 miles off Cape Finisterre, Spain, and sailing east would cross the normally busy shipping lanes. There was nothing to do except lay down in the bottom of the boat and watch the stars swaying backwards and forwards with the movement of the boat. With Bert being slim he was able to crawl up into the bow of the boat so that only half of his body was exposed to the night air which seemed very damp and cold. When the ship had been torpedoed he only managed to grab his life jacket and now he cursed for not grabbing some warm clothes. He was dressed in only a shirt, a pair of jeans and sandals without socks. However he felt great because he was still alive and besides what a great adventure to tell everyone when he arrived home. The first night seemed endless and he slept in fits and starts.

It was great when the sun came up and he sat up to look at the other boats. What a shock he received, the ocean was empty. They were all alone. Somehow during the night the other three boats had made better speed and slipped away without them being missed. Later Bert's companions learned that a French ship had picked them up after four days and taken them to Casablanca.

The lifeboat provisions consisted of two very small barrels of water. Hard tack — biscuits that appeared to be made of wood and no doubt were. Bully beef which could not be eaten because it was too salty and made the survivors more thirsty. A small bottle of brandy, or maybe it was rum, Bert could not tell at his tender age, and a few tins of condensed milk to be diluted in the ration of water. The water ration itself was the water dipper that was lowered through the small bung hole in the barrel and was about four inches in length. Each man received this issue three times a day. Bert estimated that it was the equivalent of an egg cup of water. Maybe he exaggerated a little but it would not be by much. The third drink of the day in the evening would be spliced with a little of the spirits and although never a drinker, Bert always swears that it helped to keep him alive.

As the days wore on and the thirst became more acute, no matter how he tried, he could not stop himself thinking of the water taps he knew in Liverpool. He would force himself to stop thinking of one tap only to think of one in another location. It was strange to him because in normal times he would never drink water.

The days were just as long as the nights and he really did miss having someone to talk to. He was only a "kid" and was never brought into conversation. In later years he would read about men in lifeboats being led by a strong personality who would keep up morale and make sure the survivors exercised every day. Unfortunately there was no leadership in their boat and maybe he often thinks that this was the reason for them becoming adrift from the other boats.

The days were very calm and there was little wind, in fact their sail hung limp most times. The only thing of interest to be seen were occasional jellyfish, called the Portuguese man-of-war. They were very colourful and had an inflated sail that allowed them to skud across the water with the help of any breeze.

On the fourth day some of the men claimed to have seen a U-boat. This was a worry because out there no one knew of their presence and the U-boat commander could have been a sadist as so many of them were. It would be so easy to use them for target practice or even ram them, just for the fun of it. Bert held his breath, but after a couple of hours, felt safe once more. However this now was a sobering thought, they were at the mercy of any cruel U-boat captain and just hoped that they would not be spotted before they were "picked up".

Thursday and their fifth day in the boat and things were looking a little grim. They could tell by the absence of a wake that they were making no progress. The weather was quite hot during the day and cool at night. Their water supply was giving cause for alarm. One barrel being empty and the other one with its level falling rapidly. Bert had a silly thought that he kept to himself. What if they had drifted down the Portuguese coast and somehow sailed through the Straits of Gibraltar at night? They could now be sailing up the middle of the Mediterranean Sea and would eventually all die of thirst.

Thursday was his worst day; the one day he remembers where he actually felt despair. Sailing you felt that you were getting somewhere, but drifting seemed so soul-destroying. Thursday night did not help his flagging spirits either. He had tried to sleep to blot out his surroundings when a big Australian AB squeezed in beside him and became amorous. Bert in anger and revulsion used his elbows and knees to warn off this man; embarrassment and the fact he was one of their mates, prevented him from complaining. However he sat up for the rest of the night too afraid to lay down and sleep.

In the early hours of Friday he decided that the great adventure was over now it had become serious — it was time to pray and pray real hard. He had heard of miracles but never had he believed in them; however even as he prayed, a no doubt very disjointed prayer, the wind sprang up and filled the sail. The boat surged forward as if driven by an engine. It blew all Friday and the seas rose. However what did it matter if some of the seas came in over the side? At nightfall they ran into rain squalls. Canvass was laid out in the hopes of collecting the water but unfortunately it tasted salty. The men's spirits seemed to lift and they even talked to Bert. The handling of the tiller at times took two men. They must have had a following sea, because the boat seemed to be surfing. Saturday came and it was still blowing quite hard. The sky was very overcast and grey but all knew they were going home. By midnight on the Saturday night a land light was clearly visible sending out its flashing light. To celebrate, the second mate decided to let the men finish off the water, but as it turned out they were still fourteen hours from safety and stepping on land once again.

The sea was quite choppy as they approached land and the spray that kept wetting them was like ice. Even with this discomfort, their spirits remained elated.

At daybreak they could see land in the distance and sea birds flew overhead as if to welcome them.

The Sunday morning dragged on and Bert was getting impatient now. Surely eight days to sail to land was enough without the time "dragging" on now that they could see it? Approaching the time of one-thirty, they could clearly see the breakers as they came round the headland. It was then that the second mate decided to fire their distress flares. It was no good having survived this far only to drown in the surf. Soon after the flares exploded in the sky, figures could be plainly seen running down the beach and then launching boats. It was a wonderful sight and one that Bert would never forget. In no time at all they were alongside the lifeboat and some of their helpers who were fishermen, jumped into the boat and took up the oars. Quickly they were through the surf and eager hands were helping them out of the boat. Bert found himself in the arms of a stout fisherman who carried him through a crowd of crying fishermen's wives. As they passed the women, they wailed "Poor little Anglais boy" in a broken English and wanted to stroke his face in a motherly fashion. Like their husbands they were very pro-British and closely akin to the sea. The place that the boat had finally taken them to was a Portuguese holiday resort called Figueira Da Foz. It was halfway down the Portuguese coast, proving that they had drifted south for quite a few days; in fact they had sailed 500 miles instead of what should have been 350 miles.

Once on land, they were taken to an ocean-front hotel and supplied with refreshments. They were shocked to learn that the British Army had been evacuated from Dunkirk and their extreme tiredness made it impossible to comprehend this news.

Chapter 4

Portugal and the *Ulster Prince*

Sleeping the sleep of the dead without dreams, they were brought back from oblivion to be given the dubious kindness of haircuts and shaves at midnight. Bert has often wondered the reason for this and his only conclusion is the Portuguese were checking to see if they were still alive. They were allowed to return to their beds once the barber had finished with them.

At nine next morning, feeling on top of the world, they were advised that hot baths were awaiting them. This then was luxury and all the discomfort of the past week was being pushed to the back of their memories. They were alive and in the hands of people who cared. Breakfast was waiting and to see among other things on the table the various fruit drinks made Bert want to pinch himself after the meagre water ration that they had just experienced.

Later on that morning they were taken in charge of the British authorities and taken north to Oporto. They were placed in a hotel far from comparison with their first hotel. The locals later told the men that it was a brothel that had been turned over to accommodate them. It would be better not to dwell on the shoddy treatment received from the British authorities, but rather remember the extreme kindness shown to them by the British expatriates most of whom were in the port wine business. These wine producers, shippers and exporters, rallied round the destitute seamen providing clothes and entertainment for them, when not a penny was supplied from the Embassy.

Bert had terrible trouble with his feet and should really have been taken to the hospital. His feet swelled like soccer balls and naturally he could not wear shoes or sandals. One of the seamen took him to the Embassy to try and get him some medical help. They waited for their turn at the counter only to be told by the official, that they were far too busy to worry about doctors or hospitals. The seaman

29

told the official that this boy has just spent eight days in a lifeboat, but the official remained unmoved.

Leaving the Embassy, they vowed to write to the press when they arrived home, but both were so happy to arrive back in the UK with their families, it is doubtful if they gave it a thought. On their way back to their hotel they had to pass the German Embassy, flying a huge swastika. It flew from three storeys up to nearly ground level. As a joke the seamen said to Bert, "I bet if we were to go in there you would receive medical treatment."

One morning there was a terrible to-do. The ex-RN gunner was threatening to "do" all and sundry. It was a fearful sight to see a normally quiet man so enraged. It so happened that he took size thirteen in shoes and the British expatriates had managed to purchase the only size thirteen shoes in Oporto for him. He had worn them once and then during the night someone had slipped into his room and taken them. Had he found the person responsible for taking them, it is doubtful if that person would have lived long enough to enjoy his ill-gotten goods.

Every afternoon, the seamen were taken for afternoon tea to a different house, by these kindly Britishers. A much-appreciated visit to Graham's Winery had Bert returning to the hotel with a funny head and dizzy. According to the "experts", the seamen, the port was delightful. Each man was given a small bottle of what was reputed to be the second finest port money could buy. The seamen soon drank their bottles but Bert secreted his from them so that he could take the bottle home for his father.

Besides being taken to the local cinema, one night they were taken to a wonderful fireworks display. It seemed very appropriate, because when they arrived back at their hotel they were told that they would be leaving the following night for Lisbon, where a ship was waiting to take them back to Britain.

Departure time came and they boarded the train a little sadly. Their stay had been made so pleasant by a wonderful group of British people. Once again, on boarding the train, they found that the Embassy had run true to form in placing them in a carriage crowded with peasants and their livestock. There was no complaint about these good-hearted generous people who were prepared to share their food with the seamen; but the goats, sheep and geese; the farmyard smells throughout the night were truly on the nose. The rail trip did have its moments of interest during the early morning daylight hours, such as seeing country women doing their washing in the various streams along the route, using large stones to beat the clothes against the rocks. It has always puzzled Bert, how the clothes survived this treatment.

Mid-morning saw them arrive in Lisbon, bleary-eyed, dishevelled and hungry. They had not eaten since the evening meal the day before, and having no money to spend, could not even buy a drink. They were taken immediately to the docks where they were taken aboard a most familiar ship to Bert. The *Ulster Prince* was an old favourite of his having seen her sail hundreds of times to Belfast from the Liverpool landing stage. This was the first time that he had been on board her, but it felt as if he was already home. They were taken to the dining saloon and given a good meal and then he received a further surprise by meeting her captain, Captain Wilson, a one-time neighbour of his family when they lived at Allerton. He was equally shocked to meet Bert and wanted to know how the "wee boy" had come to be in Lisbon boarding his ship.

Once Bert was settled in his cabin, Captain Wilson sent for him and he had to relate to all the events that had culminated with him being on the *Ulster Prince*. Captain Wilson was a grand Ulsterman and his crew thought the world of him. In fact one of the crew confided in Bert that the crew would sail to hell with him knowing that he would get them back again. These words were very prophetic, because the *Ulster Prince* more or less sailed to hell and back, for hundreds of wounded soldiers at Anzio in Italy, during her stint later in the war as a hospital ship. It was only great captaincy that saved the game little ship during a terrible bombing attack.

The *Ulster Prince* had been sent to Lisbon in the hope of bringing home any Britishers, whether they be military or civilian, after the evacuation of Dunkirk.

The *Ulster Prince* sailed from Lisbon on Bert's seventeenth birthday, which happened to be American Independence Day, the 4th July. Off the coast, an American cruiser was celebrating by firing all her guns. Bert likes to imagine that the cannonade was in his honour. Once at sea the ex-*Wellington Star* crew joined with the deck crew of the *Ulster Prince* in keeping "lookout watches". Bert was able to volunteer for the first time with the other seamen. Thursday and Friday were uneventful as they crossed the Bay of Biscay.

On the Saturday morning however, a U-boat was sighted but they changed course and with their superior speed were able to escape. Late in the afternoon, approaching Land's End and with the land close by, a German bomber came over from the land and dropped a stick of bombs, missing the stern by an estimated fifteen feet. Bert was resting on his bunk after completing his volunteer watch-keeping. The cabin was a peacetime steerage cabin and was situated in the stern of the ship. Once again, he had had a close call.

As he raced up the stairs to the deck, the alarm bells sounded; but he was aware that the *Ulster Prince* was a sitting duck; her armaments being a few Lewis guns fastened on ropes, like washing hanging on clotheslines.

Everyone on board were given the thrill of seeing a Hurricane fighter streaking across the sky after the bomber and then a British destroyer speeding out to meet them, showing a great "white bone in her teeth" (a beautiful large bow wave, a testimony to her high speed).

Once Land's End had been passed, there were no further incidents and they sailed on in lovely summer weather through the rest of the Saturday and throughout Sunday. Captain Wilson informed Bert that their destination was the Clyde. It would have been better if it had been the Mersey, but what the heck, they were nearly home. It was grand sailing up the Firth of Clyde with a setting sun astern of them and the smell of heather wafting across the water from the hills. As they moored to the wharf in Greenock, Bert never felt happier, he was indeed home.

Monday came, and the seamen were given rail vouchers to their various destinations. Bert left Glasgow on the 4.30 p.m. train and arrived at the Exchange Station in Liverpool at 10.30 p.m. His father and his youngest uncle were there to greet him.

A week later he had to meet with the full crew of the *Wellington Star* at the Shipping Federation Office in Paradise Street, Liverpool, to officially "sign off". He was amazed to receive the sum of eleven pounds, nineteen shillings and ten pence; his total amount earned from the 2nd March to the exact minute that they had been torpedoed. Together with the allotments left for his mother and his Health and Unemployment Stamps, the grand sum of his wages were £22-13-5. It came as quite a shock to find that all the hardships and danger that they had just endured, were at their own expense, in their own time.

Chapter 5

Time Ashore

Bert found it necessary to stay ashore for two years after his experience in the lifeboat. He obtained work as a clerk at the Olive Mount Children's Hospital, Childwall. Shortly after his arrival home the air raids started. Strangely enough, the first time the sirens were to sound warning of the approach of a German bomber, was during a visit to Captain Wilson's wife at Allerton. The plane dropped bombs over on the Wirral but it was a sign of things to come for the people of Liverpool. Many a night he was to wish that he was back at sea, because in spite of his experience he felt safer with water underneath him.

In the November, the family home in Aigburth, was wrecked by a landmine that completely demolished a whole row of houses in the next road, killing about fifty people. His mother, father and two sisters were sheltering under the stairs and he was sitting on the floor in the kitchen corner. Both of these positions were said to be the safest places in a house, during a raid. By a freakish blast, one of the chrome candlesticks standing on the mantelpiece, had been cut in half. At the same time, a fall of soot had been swept round the corner, burying Bert up to his neck. After the first trauma of thinking that he was covered in blood, the family laughed uncontrollably with relief.

When daylight came, they were all appalled at the damage about them and thanked God that they were the lucky ones to survive. Their luck held out, even to the extent of having no home and yet finding another house just one mile away to rent. With the belongings salvaged from their wrecked home, they were able to start again. Later this house was badly damaged by delayed action bombs, but they were fortunate this time, in not having to move out.

The "Eight Nights' Blitz" saw Merseyside in a sore and sorry state. The heart was virtually blasted and burned out of the city. Shocking damage was done to the docks and warehouses. A munition ship, the *Malakand*, was set on fire by blazing dock sheds in the Huskisson number 2 dock. The resulting explosion obliterated the whole area. This night the 4th May 1941, was to remain forever in the memory of Merseysiders. During that Saturday night of horror, a munition train also blew up at the Breck siding. Throughout the night there were heavy explosions heard throughout the city as each truck blew up. People had little sleep in those terrible days and yet would never dream of taking a day off work.

One morning, soon after the raids eased off, Bert's father announced that he was joining the Army. He was thirty-nine years of age and in a reserved occupation, but felt that now was the time to hit back at Hitler. This summed up the anger of the people over the terrible casualties suffered by the civilian population; young, old, infirmed, female or male. People would look round at each other and wonder who would die that night.

When Bert's father went away, he too started to get itchy feet. He visited the recruiting office in Renshaw Street, Liverpool and volunteered for the Royal Navy. However he failed the "medical" — something about a heart murmur.

This was an indignity, because he now had a girlfriend; one of the nurses at Olive Mount. Hilda was well thought of as a nurse and was much sought after by the young chaps still not called-up; she lived in Higher Tranmere across the river. On her nights off, they would travel across the Mersey by ferry to one of the many cinemas in Liverpool. During this time they probably saw more action than a lot of the troops overseas. Enemy planes diving down, machine-gunning searchlights that held them in their beam. Blazing buildings, the crunch of bombs and the whistle of falling bombs; not forgetting the ever present danger of mines as they crossed the river by ferry.

At the end of 1941 he had had enough. Having gained entry into the Merchant Navy in 1940, there would be nothing to stop him re-entering the service. This time however it would be different, he would enter to do something worthwhile and warrant some respect. He well remembered the silly fights with the seamen on the *Wellington Star* over rations, etc.

Early in 1942, he enrolled at the Liverpool Wireless College, to be trained as a radio officer. It was hard going, working during the day and attending the school at night. Then there was fire-watch duty once a week at the hospital and against his bosses wishes he had joined the Home Guard and so once every eight days had to stand guard at a strategic point. To add to this crammed itinerary, he managed to fit in enjoyable nights out with Hilda. Looking back after the war he wondered how he ever managed to fit all his commitments in.

Later in the year, he received a generous offer from the wireless school, to attend day school at no extra cost and they would pay him for attending night school and help out with tuition. He had a suspicion that this offer was made through the intervention of his father's army welfare officer. Leaving his job at the hospital he took up the offer.

Passing his PMG Radio Officer's Certificate before the Christmas, he was offered a full-time job by the school principal, but turned it down because the spirit of adventure was still in his blood. He also felt that he was as yet not fully qualified without sea service. The certificate he had just passed was a special wartime edition to enable ships to keep round the clock listening watches. After six months at sea the operator could go ashore and pass his full second-class peacetime certificate.

Allowing himself the luxury of Christmas at home, he approached the Bibby Line in the last week of the old year for a position on their seagoing staff. Their ships in peacetime were named after English counties and sailed between the UK and India and Burma. The British Army had used these ships for many years as troop carriers. One special characteristic they had, that made them easy to pick out was, they had four masts. The deck and cabin crews were Indian or similar nationality. Bibby's shipping superintendent promised Bert a position when one became available.

Late afternoon, on the 9th January, he received a telegram to report by 9 p.m. to the *Empire Pride* in the Langton Dock. He was to have taken Hilda out that night and was to have met her at the Central Underground Station at 7 p.m.; he realised he could still see her if she was not late and then catch a tram to the Langton Dock. There was no other way that he could contact her. Fortunately she was early and was able to farewell him at the tram stop.

Boarding a tram to the docks he had that old familiar "brick" in the stomach. The name of the ship puzzled him because he could not associate it with the Bibby Line.

Arriving at the Langton Dock he made his way gingerly through dock sheds and other obstacles common to docks. The blackout conditions made it impossible without a moon to take in the area, let alone see his new ship. His thoughts went back to that night over two years ago when he found himself floundering through unfamiliar countryside looking for the *Vindicatrix*. He felt much older now and yet he still had those same old thoughts. This time however he was fully aware of what was out there because this time he had experience. Finally he was alongside a ship and on closer scrutiny he realised it was the *Empire Pride*. Climbing the unlit gangway he was happy to enter the bridge area with its lights that could not be seen from outside.

Chapter 6

The *Empire Pride*

Signing on immediately, he was introduced to other officers and then shown to his cabin. It was quite comfortable and modern. Talking to the second purser, who became a firm friend, he was given a few facts about the ship. She was comparatively new, replacing another Bibby Line ship sunk by enemy action. This explained the name *Empire Pride*; wartime built ships were named "Empire". She was of 9,000 tons and had a Doxford diesel engine giving her a speed of 16 knots. Her "lines" were quite ugly, but to offset this, she was one of those ships that seemed to be blessed with luck. She carried 2,500 troops packed in quarters like sardines and slept in hammocks. Evidently she had been fitted out purely as a troopship. Conditions for the army officers were completely different than that of the ordinary ranks. They shared the comfortable conditions of the deck officers' dining saloon and the excellent cuisine. Bert soon realised that it was worth all his efforts to become a junior officer in the Merchant Navy, if only from the point of view of the food and conditions. It was great to have a steward to "do" for you instead of being the whipping boy for a crowd of "rough necks".

Shortly after 10 p.m. he could feel the ship vibrating and was surprised to find her moving out into the river, where she was taken in tow by tugs and taken to the Liverpool landing stage. This was where as a boy, he had stood so many times, watching great liners come and go. During the next two days they embarked their 2,500 troops and supplies. Bert enjoyed watching the troops in high spirits, playing practical jokes on one another to pass the time away. He wondered how they felt as individuals. Did they think that this could be their last contact with their homeland? Some no doubt would not be returning.

Immediately on leaving the Mersey, spaces started appearing at

37

the various tables seating the army officers. Two or three meals later there were only a handful of hardy souls. Once the missing officers started returning, they were well into the Atlantic. One thing Bert realised very quickly on leaving the landing stage was that the *Empire Pride* was a beauty at rolling and consequently creaking. This gave him a lot of heart because an old sailor had once told him good ships creaked a lot. The tablecloths were nearly always wet at sea to prevent the dishes sliding onto the deck. Square frames were also used to divide the table tops into smaller areas, so as to give the smallest amount of movement to the dishes.

The worst feature of the *"Pride"* was his lifeboat. It was situated well aft and there was no way he could reach it through so many troops lined up at their respective boats. When they had lifeboat drill he found that by racing down the companionway stairs, he could pass alongside the entrance to the engine room and then up another set of stairs until once again he could reach the boat deck near his boat. He confided in his new friend the second purser that if they were torpedoed he would go straight over the side and swim for it. There was no way that he would go down inside the ship to get to a lifeboat.

The convoy that they sailed to Gibraltar with, would have been worth "plucking" had there been U-boats in the vicinity. They were the smallest troop transport and yet the thousands of men arrived safely. He was told to go ashore in Gibraltar with the second sparks and pick up the ship's mail at the RN mail office. The motor lifeboat taking them from their anchorage passed close to various ships riding at anchor. One, an American liberty ship had an enormous hole in her side that looked big enough to drive three locomotives through side by side.

Leaving Gibraltar they were all keyed up and ready for action. However considering the size and importance of the convoy, their passage was a peaceful one. Algiers was reached and made a lovely sight as they sailed round the headland. It stood out so white against the blue of the sea and sky. Looking across at one of the sandy beaches was a large freighter that had been beached to stop it sinking after it had been torpedoed or mined. This was a sobering thought as they sailed into the Port of Algiers on a beautiful sunny afternoon.

Once moored inside the dock area, the troops commenced to disembark. Bert and the second sparks were once again given the pleasant task of walking to the mail office for the ship's mail. Once ashore he was to find that what appeared so beautiful from the sea was not all beauty when amongst it. There were fine buildings and very fine tree-lined streets, but there was also the casbah with its seedy buildings and narrow passageways, most of which was out of bounds to the troops and anybody else with sense. Returning to the ship they were told that they were sailing back to the UK the next morning.

Dinner was at 7 p.m. and the ship's officers had virtually the dining saloon to themselves. Having just dispatched the soup, they were about to be served the main course, when without warning there was the most violent explosion that seemed to lift the ship out of the water. Bert fully expected to see the sea come pouring in on them, but as it happened they had come through a bombing attack unscathed. Evidently a large bomb had been dropped alongside them without doing any damage. It was rather a shaken group that continued with their dinner.

The return trip to the UK was just as peaceful as the outward bound trip and had given Bert the chance to settle down once again to seaboard life as third sparks. He made friends with everyone except his chief radio officer, who seemed to have a terrible chip on his shoulder. Whatever had happened to him had made him scared stiff of the captain. Bert found that there was no pleasing him and kept out of his way as much as possible.

Arriving in the Firth of Clyde they were told to proceed to the Gareloch, where they were to anchor and take on troops. The troops would be taken out by tender from Faslane.

On the Sunday morning, a few of the crew were allowed ashore for a couple of hours at a little village called Helensburgh. The lifeboat was lowered for their transportation ashore and Bert was delighted at being offered a trip with them. Once ashore he felt the urge to speak to his mother on the phone; however they were not on the phone at home. With a lot of co-operation from the telephone people and a newsagent's shop about one and a half miles from his home, his mother was brought to the phone. Such things could only happen in wartime — people really cared. It was great to hear his mother's voice but when he rang off he realised that he was in trouble. Negotiations for the call had taken so long, the time had long since gone when he should have rejoined the returning crew members in the lifeboat. Trying not to panic he was relieved when a boat came in from another ship, the *Sobenski*, a Polish liner that was to join their convoy. Bert cajoled his way into getting a lift back to the *"Pride"*, but when they drew alongside the Polish ship their chief officer shouted down to the boat crew that they were not to take Bert back to his ship. Bert did not fancy swimming in the icy water and shouted back "Well I can hardly swim." To his relief the officer relented and he was taken over to the *"Pride"*. Once on board he was left wondering if the officer had really been serious.

Just prior to sailing, Bert gave a shore worker a parcel of fruit to post to his family. To cover the postage cost, he handed over a five-pound note; this he knew would more than pay for the stamps and allow the worker to buy himself a few drinks. However he did not know at the time how much trouble this gesture would cause him, together with a letter that he posted by ship's mail, to his mother.

Once again the *"Pride"* was to prove how Dame Fortune was to always favour her. The convoy arrived in Algiers without even a scare. Owing to the number of ships in port the *Empire Pride* had to disembark her troops from her anchorage; tenders taking the troops ashore. Shore leave was given to some of the crew and once again the motor lifeboat was used. The last arranged service to the ship was waiting at the wharf with the captain sitting sedately on one of the thwarts. At precisely the time arranged for them to leave, the fourth mate gave the order to "cast off". Suddenly the native crew became very excited and pointed to a figure doing his best to reach them in a hurry. The captain turned and said to the mate "You had better wait for him". As the straggler climbed into the boat he threw up over one of the crew's head. Everyone thought that the captain was going to have a fit. There and then he gave the order "The dirty so-and-sos are to be back on board, before I am picked up, in future." It was a most repulsive incident, especially with them going back to the ship for dinner.

The *"Pride"* was due to sail for the UK the next afternoon. As they lay at anchor the next morning there was a most remarkable incident. The air seemed to vibrate with a pulsating angry aircraft engine sound. Running out on deck, Bert was fascinated by an aircraft coming down in tight circles. He stood amazed at the cleverness of the pilot, until he suddenly realised it was for real; the plane was crashing into the sea. As it hit the water a great plume of water rose up and then it was gone. It left him with a funny feeling in his stomach when he realised that there had been men inside that plane when it hit the sea. Later he was told that it was a German Junkers 88 and had evidently been shot down by an allied plane, because there had been no anti-aircraft fire.

The *Moreton Bay*, another troop transport, proved how unpredictable life at sea was in wartime. The *"Pride"* was preparing to join her convoy when news was signalled to her to go alongside to embark the *Moreton Bay*'s troops. Evidently as she was leaving the dock side, one of her mooring ropes fouled her propeller. This indeed was a blow, because the destination of the *Moreton Bay* had been Bone, only ninety miles from the front line. Every ship or convoy that had sailed along that part of the coast had been heavily attacked by E-boats, U-boats and aircraft. Once the troops were re-embarked the *"Pride"* took on the pilot and she pulled out into the bay to join her escorts. The escorts turned out to be two peacetime cross-channel ferries. They were fast, but all on board the *"Pride"* wondered how they would cope with a U-boat; however they seemed well equiped with anti-aircraft guns. Having so many troops on board and taking them so near the front, was a big responsibility for all on board the *"Pride"*. They were full of apprehension from the time they left Algiers.

Nearing Bone, they could clearly see a supply convoy being heavily attacked by torpedo bombers. They sailed on and skirted the slower convoy with bated breath. For some strange reason they sailed into the harbour of Bone without a direct attack on them. As they reached the harbour mole they had to sail past an American tanker that had been bombed four days before and was still burning. The ill-fated ship had been on her maiden voyage.

The instant the *"Pride"* drew alongside, a destroyer pulled alongside her and announced that it was her guard ship. With the wireless blackout in port, the operators were always at a loose end after having made a check of their emergency batteries. This was no exception and Bert took the opportunity to stroll round the empty boat deck. As he wandered up and down he could still hear the guns and see the flashes as the guns were fired from the convoy being attacked. Looking up over the dock area he became aware of an object in the sky that filled him with horror. There appeared to be the largest bomb that could be imagined. The fading light gave it a grotesque appearance. Standing rooted to the spot, he was holding his breath when the object rolled over and he could see that it was a naval barrage balloon that had been punctured, no doubt with shrapnel. He started to sweat with relief, because having survived the bombing raids on Merseyside, he had thought that it was one of those terrible land mines.

Next morning and they were at sea again, heading back to Algiers a much relieved crew. Once again good fortune had smiled on the *"Pride"*. It was strange how one's confidence could grow in a ship and Bert felt safe and at home in her.

Algiers and then Gibraltar were reached without drama and then she was ordered to the Azores under the protection of two corvettes. They ran into heavy weather shortly after leaving "Gib" and even on the big ship, conditions were uncomfortable. Conditions on the escort vessels must have been intolerable as they kept taking water over their decks. Their commanders kept asking for a reduction in speed until finally the *"Pride"* told them that she could no longer reduce speed because she would lose steering way. Eventually a message was received from the Admiralty telling them to turn back to Gibraltar as a U-boat pack was in the vicinity. They were advised to make a run for it at their best possible speed. It was a dramatic situation wondering how long it would be before a torpedo tore their hull open. However once again they reached the safety of Gibraltar by themselves. Joining a homeward bound convoy, Bert was delighted to hear that their destination was Liverpool.

Once safely moored to the Liverpool landing stage, he was able to slip away to his home in Aigburth, with his friend the second purser. Returning to the ship two and a half hours later, they were fortunate to be able to go aboard. A gale had sprung up and the *"Pride"* was riding violently against the pontoons between her and the landing stage. The deck hands were preparing to cast off so that she could anchor in mid-stream. She was taken out into the river with the help of tugs and anchored off Cammel Lairds Shipbuilding Yard. She was to wait for just over two days for the gale to abate.

Next morning Bert was to be shocked with the incident that unknown to him had started with the fruit parcel and letter from the Gareloch. In the first place, his mother had not received the fruit; evidently the shore worker had kept the fruit and the money. The letter that had been sent with the ship's mail had been censored and where he had mentioned that if they went back to where they had just been, he would try to send more fruit — evidently whoever had censored the mail (mostly it was army officers in hospital) had thought that it was some sort of coded message. He was summoned to the captain's cabin and was surprised to see his chief radio officer already in the cabin.

Entering the cabin he was immediately accosted by the captain wanting to know what he had written and not waiting for an explanation went on to threaten Bert with gaol. Bert in a shocked state of mind tried desperately to remember what he had actually written, because he did not consider himself an idiot to write in mail, shipping movements. Gradually it came back to him and he tried to remember exactly what he in fact had written so that the captain would understand. The captain listened and then said to him "You must have written more than that." Not once did his boss come to his aid and appeared to want to crucify him. He kept saying like a parrot "I have told him repeatedly about the Secrets Act and I have warned him about this and that, sir." Bert felt sick, it was bad enough being blamed for something you knew you were innocent of, without having a slimy individual wanting to bury you. He was telling unnecessary lies to protect himself when there was reason to. Bert kept clenching his fist trying to get control of himself, because he felt like punching him in the mouth. They were finally dismissed with Bert feeling like throwing up at the gutless individual who was his boss. There and then he decided to leave the ship as soon as they docked.

With the gale abating they received a message from the shipyard that they were waiting to launch a ship from the slipway and how soon could they move? For Bert it could not come quickly enough because in spite of his various friends offering their regrets and comfort, he felt very upset. They were taken into the Huskisson Dock with the afternoon tide and Bert promptly signed off the ship. The second sparks also signed off to attend a family wedding and take leave that was owing.

As they left the ship, the second struggled with his case and a rather large deep box with home-made rope handles. Bert helped him the best way that he could because he also had his own "gear". Approaching the policeman on gate duty the second asked where the nearest phone was because he wanted to ring for a taxi. On being given the instructions he asked the PC if he would watch over his belongings. Bert wondered about this and thought even after three months, he does not trust me. The wooden box appeared to be full of fruit and the PC turned to Bert and said "My little girl would be thrilled with a banana, she has never seen one." Bert told him to ask for one, because there was so much fruit; one banana would not be missed. On his return the PC told him about his little daughter and promptly received half a bunch of the fruit. Eventually the taxi came and once under way Bert asked the second the reason for him asking the PC to keep an eye on his belongings. For answer the second reached forward into the wooden box and pushed aside the fruit, underneath were bottles of Vat 69 whisky, duty-free from the ship. He was evidently an old hand at these tricks and explained that if you wanted to take anything ashore, you just drew attention to it in a matter-of-fact way, the way that he had done. He explained that it was for the wedding because it was virtually impossible to get whisky ashore. Bert told him that if he had known what was in the box he would not have waited for him. The second replied, "I know, that is why I did not confide in you, you would have given the game away."

When he arrived home his family were surprised to see him, because when he did not arrive the day after his visit, they thought that he had gone back to sea.

Chapter 7

MT *Thorhild*

The turning point in Bert's seagoing career came with him leaving the *Empire Pride*. He had one week to make up his mind whether to apply to another shipping company or join the Merchant Navy Reserve Pool and let them find him another ship. The latter was a gamble because you could not pick and choose the type of ship, the nationality, or in some cases the destination. Chances were you find yourself on the hell run to Murmansk, Russia. He finally decided to gamble and take whatever came up with the "Pool" because he did not want to spend his leave chasing from one shipping line to another. There was never a long wait for a ship because seafarers were at a premium.

He wondered whether he had made the right decision, when the family received news that a distant relation of his mother had been lost aboard a tanker. Evidently it had blown up with all hands in the North Atlantic. He too had been a radio officer.

One fear Bert had, was being on board a ship bound for Russia. The intense cold frightened him. A mate of his had served on board a destroyer on the Russian run and had told him about the very brave Hurricane fighter pilots that were catapulted off merchant ships. Once in the air they had nowhere to land except bale out and land in the sea. The destroyer would lower a boat and then had two minutes to retrieve the pilot before he froze to death. Many times the pilot would wave to the boat's crew and be dead when they reached him. Bert thought that these men, together with the men of the bomb disposal squad, were the bravest men that ever lived.

Bert received a telegram from the "Pool" on the 22nd April, the day before Good Friday, advising him to join the MT *Thorhild* immediately in the West Float Dock, Bidston. He had been keeping his fingers crossed that he would have Easter at home, but evidently that was not to be.

44

Taking an underground railway train from Liverpool Central Station, he journeyed to the Bidston Station. Walking from the railway he could see the dock but not the ship. Turning a bend in the dock road he saw her. First impressions were one of pleasant surprise. She was evidently modern with nice lines for a tanker, and Norwegian. Boarding her was a strange sensation; as he left the gangway, he felt that he was on the top of the Dingle oil tanks. It gave him the creeps at the thought of living on top of so much oil.

Entering the captain's lounge room, he signed articles and was told to return the next day to take up his duties. He stayed long enough to ask a few questions about her. She was 10,000 tons, registered in Oslo and had sailed to Britain when the Germans invaded Norway. From that time on she had been carrying oil from the USA to Britain. The chief sparks was a young Canadian, who unlike his last boss, made Bert most welcome; so much so, they became good friends. The second sparks was a Norwegian called Joachim; quite a character and was to share a lovely cabin with Bert. In peacetime the *Thorhild* had carried a staff captain and his lovely cabin was given over to the two sparks. It was luxury to look out of two windows from the settee instead of two small portholes.

Sailing from the Mersey the next day in a severe thunderstorm, Bert could not help but wonder what the future had in store for him. As they sailed past New Brighton, he wondered if they would see it again, because he had heard so much about tankers being the U-boats' prime targets. Everything on board seemed to be impregnated with oil, even a glass of water. He wondered if he would ever get used to the smell of oil.

As they joined up with over one hundred other ships to form a west-bound convoy, he little realised that this was the beginning of seven and a half very happy months for him. The Norwegians were a very good crew to sail with and certainly took pride in their ship. It was their home for the duration and they knew how to look after it. The huge tank deck, with its mass of pipes and pumphouse, was a credit to them. You would find no rust on this ship — painted a rich green, like a beautiful field. Bert actually fell in love with her, because unlike cargo ships she had an easy rolling motion — long slow rolls. If there was a drawback it was at meal times; the officers (not including the captain) shared the engineers' mess, which was aft. It was quite pleasant, walking to the mess along the catwalk, in fine weather, but it was very uncomfortable in a North Atlantic gale with seas sweeping over the tank deck. It was a case of watching the seas and then trying to run between the troughs in the waves.

Two or three days out from Liverpool, Bert became used to the oil smell and the oil taste. This in itself helped him to settle down to his strange surroundings. Leaving the UK, the *Thorhild* would take aboard sea water in her tanks for ballast. On reaching the Grand Banks of Newfoundland, she would commence to pump out the water ready for taking on oil in New York.

Cigarettes were very cheap on board, at twelve shillings for eight hundred. They were American Camel and Lucky Strike, much favoured by the Norwegians. His one gripe was that they drank coffee instead of tea. Every second day at 'smoko' in the afternoon, there would be a pot of tea for a change; much appreciated by Bert. This changed however when Bert met the captain's steward, a chap that had been a class lower than his at Granby Street School. They became good shipboard friends and Frank "acquired" a silver teapot, together with a good supply of tea, sugar and condensed milk, which was secreted in Bert's cabin. From then on it was tea when ever it took their fancy.

The trip to New York was surprisingly quiet. Once in a while, two or three destroyers would converge on a spot in the ocean and drop a pattern of depth charges. They reminded Bert of bloodhounds, but whether there was a U-boat there, he had no way of knowing.

Fourteen days out from the Mersey they dropped anchor off the Bayonne Oil Terminal. The first night he was not allowed ashore by the port authorities. All newcomers to the US had to be taken ashore under guard to be fingerprinted and to receive their documents which consisted of an identification card with photograph and an Alien Registration Card with a fingerprint. These documents were issued through the US Department of Justice, Immigration and Naturalization Service. The night was spent relaxing in the knowledge of being at a safe anchorage and being entertained by an American sailor of the Coastguard Service, playing his piano accordian. He was very good and played in a dance band. The few crew members not on duty and those who had decided to stay on board, were kept entertained by him well into the small hours of the morning. At 2.30 Bert wished him a good night and was quite surprised when the sailor told him that the night was only young. Evidently he was well and truly used to the nightlife of New York.

The next day Bert, with others, was taken under guard to Manhattan to the Alien Registration Office. He felt like a criminal under arrest. With the formalities over, he was free to go his own way. Meeting up with Frank they decided on a trip to a barber's shop. When it was their turn to sit in one of the many barber's chairs, they were almost evicted for refusing all the trimmings. The trimmings consisted of, shampoo, shave, face massage and manicure. The haircut cost them a goodly portion of what they had earned crossing the Atlantic. To have the trimmings would have run them into debt.

Later in the day, Bert caught a subway train to the Bronx, to visit his mother's girl friend who now lived there with her husband. Both Mary and John gave him a fabulous weekend. It was at their apartment that he became aware of the stupidity of war. Mary took him to visit her neighbours in the apartment building. Next to hers lived the sweetest old ladies; one of eighty-six years, the other ninety-two years. They were sisters and had been born in Germany. They welcomed him into their home with hugs, reminiscent of his own grandmother in England. Further down the hall was another German family friendly with Mary. There was the husband and wife together with their young children. Mary advised Bert to be careful what he said about the war, because the young couples' families were in Hamburg, which was being heavily bombed every night by the RAF. They made him very welcome and left Bert wondering what the damned war was really all about after all. The realities of death and destruction were so unreal in these apartments, whose occupants welcomed a stranger with open arms and a smile. He rejoined the *Thorhild* puzzled and with mixed feelings.

The trip home was quiet, with over one hundred ships, (freighters and tankers) loaded down with war supplies. How the German U-boats would have liked to have got among them.

Arriving in Bristol on the 30th May, and with no chance of making it to Liverpool and back, before they sailed again, Bert decided to accompany the chief sparks to London for a few hours. It would be a break from the ship and besides he had never been to London. They travelled overnight and arrived there just as the city was waking up. After a meal, a hectic round of sightseeing followed and then back on the train to Bristol.

Leaving Bristol, this convoy was to be the most boring of all the convoys he was to sail in. The Admiralty in their wisdom, and no doubt with many intelligence reports, gave them a course that took them right up into the Arctic Circle. The huge convoy of over one hundred ships and a maximum speed of seven knots had barely cleared Cape Wrath in the North West corner of Scotland, when it ran into the thickest fog imaginable. For the safety of the convoy from enemy action, this was great, but for the lookouts and navigating officers, it was a nightmare. The fog was to last for almost the entire crossing of three weeks. Fog bouys were towed astern of each vessel and the resulting plume of water was carefully followed by the ship astern. The bouy was a simple device, consisting of a hollow pipe fastened to a board. The speed of the ship forced the water up the pipe and out of the top. There could be ten or twelve lines of ships, with ten or so ships in each line. The fact that every ship was in its station when they came out of the fog three weeks later spoke volumes for the skill of the various ships' crews.

Well into the trip, Bert was surprised to hear the wireless silence broken on 600 metres, during his watch. It was the distress frequency and only an absolute emergency would cause the breaking of silence. This was one of those occasions as it turned out. A destroyer had picked up an iceberg on her radar and the convoy was heading for it. At a given signal, by hoots on the commodore's ship's siren, the entire convoy wheeled to port. As they sailed on it was a most eerie experience with ice floes crashing against the hull of the ship with a sound that seemed to reverbrate through the tanks in spite of their being filled with sea water.

The arrival in New York was always a joy to the crew. On this occasion more so after such a long miserable trip with nothing to see but part of their own ship and a blanket of fog.

Bert's joy was soon dampened when the chief sparks broke the news to him, that he was signing off the ship and going home on leave to Ontario, Canada, for some well-deserved leave. The three sparks had become firm friends and had worked well together.

The night before Harold left the ship, he went with Bert for a last night out at the Radio City Music Hall. The Yanks certainly knew how to put on entertainment. There was a double-feature film show; a live show put on by Connie Boswell the actress, and the Ink Spots. During the intermission there was an excellent organ recital. After the show they went over to Toffenetties Restaurant, Broadway and had a meal in the early hours of the morning.

That same day, Harold left the ship and Joachim was in charge. Bert was now second sparks. When they sailed again they would have to keep special watch-keeping periods to cover the most important listening times when messages were most likely to be transmitted.

Before sailing, Bert decided to take a trip to the top of the then tallest building in the world. It was 102 storeys high and it was necessary to take two lifts to the summit. Once at the top the view was fantastic and looking down the people appeared to be like ants and the cars like Dinky toys. He was most interested to see the giant

French liner the *Normandie* laying capsized on her side; the result of a huge fire caused through a welder's torch. The water pumped into her to fight the fire had caused her to capsize. It seemed so sad that such a beautiful ship should finish up like this. He had heard stories that workers were going to convert her to a giant aircraft carrier; however this could have been hearsay.

Returning to the UK, the only incident worth remembering could have had disastrous results for Bert. Spending long hours with headphones on and only the strange sounds of the ether and occasionally faint Morse signals from some unknown source, he would become drowsy. He would read books until he could hardly read the print. The ashtray would always be full of cigarette butts at the end of the watch.

One morning having retired at 4 a.m., he was called for breakfast at 7.30 a.m. ready to take over the 8 a.m. to 12 watch. First call was the toilet and then the shower. He was wearing a British army battledress given to him by his father and most invaluable in the cold North Atlantic and especially the draughty wireless room. In the toilet his hands went down to loosen his fly, but he could not feel it. Looking down he was horrified to find that the front of his trousers had disappeared. When he had pulled his pants on he had not noticed the missing material. It did not take much imagination to realise what had happened. Evidently he had been smoking and had dozed off. The cigarette causing the wool trousers to smoulder. Needless to say a very sheepish Bert disposed of the trousers over the side without anyone seeing them.

Arriving in the UK once again after another uneventful crossing, they were sent to Avonmouth to discharge their precious oil. Tanker crews seemed to be a different breed of seaman to the seamen on other vessels. It did not seem to worry them if they came in with one convoy and sailed again with the next outward bound convoy. Maybe it was the fact that they could not return to their homeland and did not worry where they were. Bert on the other hand felt so differently; he tried to go ashore at every opportunity whether it was in the UK or the US. Avonmouth was to be no different for him even though it was only a very small port. The oil jetty could not take tankers alongside and so they were moored between four bouys at the end of the jetty, with the pipes suspended over the water by means of a crane. There was no shore leave given, consequently, to which Bert seethed. He reckoned with the long hours that he and Joachim had been keeping, he could have been allowed to stretch his legs. A work's tender came alongside the

Thorhild to bring some oil workers aboard. Bert shouted to its skipper "How about taking me ashore?" to which the skipper replied, "Jump aboard." He jumped over the rail and was surprised that three or four of the *Thorhild*'s crew had joined him to go ashore. They had not travelled far when the *Thorhild*'s chief mate hailed them from the *Thorhild*'s bridge, ordering them back on board; however they all decided to pretend that they had not heard or seen him.

Once ashore and finding that it was such a quiet place, he decided to visit the local cinema. On leaving the show and with everywhere closed so that he could not buy a meal, he headed back for the dock area. He soon realised that he had a problem, there were no boats going out to the *Thorhild*, in fact the area seemed deserted.

Eventually he came across the dock master's hut and the dock master just about to leave. Bert explained his predicament and the kindly master told him that he could spend the night in the hut and he would arrange a boat to take him back the next morning. There was a camp stretcher in the hut and the master gave him a blanket.

True to his word, the harbour master woke him up with a cup of most welcome tea, and ten minutes later informed him that there was a boat waiting for him at the end of the jetty. Once on board he realised that he was not very popular with the mate, but not a lot was said. Maybe because he was English.

There were to be two more quiet trips before "Gerry" realised that they were around. However the trip after leaving Avonmouth he would never forget. Just about the entire crew came down with food poisoning. To be sick, have the "runs" and yet try and do one's duty without the help of a doctor, was beyond belief. Bert felt wretched beyond description as he asked the mate in charge of the medicines to give him a dose of "something". The mate took him into the cabin where the medicines were kept and said "Help yourself, you understand English better than me." He saw a bottle of Castor Oil and took a large dose of the foul stuff. It worked wonders and inside two hours he was well on the road to recovery.

The convoy ran into a howling gale and the seas were frightening. A convoy of well over one hundred ships would disappear from view when they were in a trough between two waves. It was inconceivable that a ship could possibly rise out of such a valley of green water. Bert often thought that they would be engulfed. Rising out of the apparent depth of the sea, the *Thorhild* would survey the horizon with all its ships as if on a mountain top. The *Thorhild* with all its 10,000 tons was made to look like a toy in the face of nature. How the crews on the rescue tug, corvettes and destroyers coped, could not be imagined. They were thrown about like corks. At least the *Thorhild* crew were dry in their quarters and had hot meals when their watch-keeping had been done.

The second day into the gale, Bert's career almost came to an end. He stepped out onto the wet deck; huge seas keeping the superstructure running with water as great waves broke over them. The wind was howling through the rigging like the death cry of a mob of banshees. With long slow rolls, the deck of the *Thorhild* was like a wet slippery dip. Unexpectedly Bert's feet started to slide and as he grabbed at a rail, so did his hands. He fell on his back and picking up speed he started to slide towards the ship's side. He knew this was going to be the end and could do nothing about it. Waking up laying on his back soaking wet with a seaman bending over him, he wondered where he was and how he had arrived in such a position. Unknown to him, some wonderful person had left the toilet door opened outwards, fastened against the bulkhead. He had slid down the deck with increasing speed and had fortunately gone under the door which together with his nose had acted as a brake. He was to be forever thankful that he was born with a prominent nose. The seaman had been crossing the catwalk and had witnessed the whole incident. He told Bert that he thought he was a "goner". A bad headache and a badly swollen nose was a small price to pay for his life.

At this stage of the war there seemed to be more danger to Bert from his own actions than by enemy action. The following trip found him in a situation that was most foolhardy to say the least. The *Thorhild* was laying off Ellis Island waiting for a homeward bound convoy, when some of the crew decided on going over the side for a swim. Bert decided to join them but unthinking dived overboard without giving a thought for the flow of the tide. As he surfaced from his dive he found he was away from the ladder and being swept further away. He was barely making headway and tiring rapidly. It was either a last-ditch effort to reach the ladder or let himself be swept away with the tide and hope that he could get hold of another ship's anchor chain. In spite of his danger he still felt embarrassment at his situation. Fear must have given him extra strength because after what seemed to be an eternity the ladder was getting nearer. Finally he was able to grab hold of it and stayed panting in spite of the water surging over him. When the ache had eased in his arms, he climbed back on board, thankful that he had survived a stupid action.

Returning to the UK after this latest incident, the *Thorhild* was advised that she was to give over so much of her tanks to fuel destroyers and other escorts. This would necessitate work being performed by a dockyard gang. Also she would have ninety depth charges clamped to her for'ard tank deck to replenish the armament of the escorts. It was decided that she would enter a graving dock and have her hull scraped and painted. This was to be carried out in Cardiff Docks after their cargo of oil had been discharged at the Swansea Oil Terminal.

Sailing up the Bristol Channel on a beautiful Saturday afternoon, Bert was due to take the last watch before docking. He strolled to the ship's side to have a few minutes' fresh air and received the shock of his life. Immediately below him, six feet from the ship's side, was a sea mine complete with horns. As he watched, fascinated, it kept its distance from the ship and finally cleared the stern. How the lookouts had not seen it was beyond belief. Eventually two minesweepers opened fire on it when it was a safe distance from the *Thorhild* exploding it in a great column of water. It seemed that Bert was the only person on board to have witnessed how close they were to disaster.

Arriving in Swansea, Bert was given one week's leave and quickly made his way to Liverpool.

The one week's leave passed all too quickly. He had enjoyed every minute of it because Hilda had been able to get one week off from the hospital and they had spent much of the time in the Wirral, their favourite beauty spot, in perfect summer weather.

Returning to the *Thorhild* at Cardiff, he felt refreshed and ready for sea again. Once in the dock area he soon found the graving dock with the *Thorhild* still high and dry. Going on board he wondered what the crew must be feeling; their pride and joy looked a mess. The frantic haste of the dockyard workers over the past week was clearly visible. Besides the untidy mess, the *Thorhild* now boasted another catwalk.

Late Sunday afternoon, with the ship looking once again like her old self, the dock was flooded and she sailed out into the Bristol Channel. As if by a sign of things to come she sailed out in a severe thunderstorm and joined her outward bound convoy. This convoy joined another two convoys; one from the Mersey, and the other from the Clyde; making a total of ninety ships. A big boost for the convoy was the presence of a Woolworth carrier. This was the first time that Bert had sailed with a carrier giving aircraft protection. This carrier was to prove priceless over the following days and added to the punch of the escort. Convoy protection was of the highest order, now, with all the latest innovations such as the *Thorhild*'s modifications and her extra supply of depth charges.

Reaching the North Atlantic, they were dismayed at being told that they were to join up with another convoy of seven knots. This was a blow because their convoy was ten knots; however the Admiralty must have received some very good intelligence of U-boat movements.

Whether it was the continuous "take-offs and landings" of the ancient Swordfish aircraft, everyone felt an air of expectancy. For twelve hours destroyers would race here and there, sometimes dropping depth charges, and at other times just making "dry runs". As close by depth charge explosions rattled through the ship, Bert could not help but be thankful that he was up on the bridge and not down in the engine room. When he had cause to go down into the engine room for distilled water for the batteries, he hated to be delayed by someone wanting to talk with him, he liked to be in and out of the engine room as quickly as possible. He still carried memories of what happened when the second torpedo hit the engine room of the *Wellington Star*.

At 2 a.m. sitting with the headphones on, he was still able to hear a loud explosion, followed by a second, two minutes later. Immediately after the second explosion, radio silence was broken and he started taking down the SSSS message from the ship next to them in the convoy. This was ship number 11. When this message was completed, ship number 15 sent her SSSS signal denoting she too had been torpedoed. The *Thorhild*'s alarm bells were ringing out, but there was precious little anyone could do except pray. There was very little darkness in the northern latitudes during summer time and it was still late summer. Bert took a quick look from the bridge and could see number 11 with her stern blown off and number 15 blown in two parts. The half that sank within two minutes contained the crew's quarters, so it was not expected many men survived. As the rescue ship and the tug sailed to aid the striken vessels, the convoy sailed on.

Throughout the 20th and 21st September, conditions were ideal for U-boats and the escort beat off many attacks. The explosion of depth charges seemed endless. During one of these attacks a lookout on the *Thorhild* reported seeing oil and bubbles coming to the surface. During one brief lull in the attacks the second mate read a message by Aldis lamp from the senior officer of the escorts to the commodore of the convoy telling him that they were being attacked by twenty U-boats. Mr Churchill was giving a speech to the world and picked up on the ship's radio saying even as he spoke a convoy in the North Atlantic was being heavily attacked by a pack of U-boats using a more powerful torpedo which was breaking ships in two. As Bert listened, it reminded him of a play, and he was one of the actors in it.

The U-boats tried a new strategy to extend their time of attack. They would race ahead of the convoy during the brighter daylight hours, surface and charge their batteries. The old Swordfish would search for them and then having found them wallow in like old ducks and attack them. However the U-boats treated them with scorn, because instead of diving they would stay on the surface and attack them with heavy AA fire. At one stage every Swordfish was grounded with damage caused by the U-boats' guns. During the twilight hours, the U-boats returned to attack, to try to snatch more merchant ships.

At 9.40 p.m. there was a tremendous explosion which had them all running out on deck. The *Thorhild* was in the front row next to the commodore's ship. Between the two ships was a ball of fire and a column of smoke. In no time there was just an awful eruption in the sea beside them. The third mate had a grandstand view of the incident, being on the bridge at the time. A Canadian destroyer (formerly a four-funnel destroyer of the US Navy) called the *San Croix*, had picked up an object in her searchlight laying between the commodore's ship and the *Thorhild*. As the third mate turned away to sound action stations, there was a violent explosion. The scene was incredible and it was obvious that the destroyer had saved the two ships, but had gone down herself. Both hunter and hunted had destroyed each other. The rescue vessel picked up one officer and seventy-six men from the destroyer, but tragically she too was torpedoed and only one man survived from the two crews. It was fatal for a ship to drop back from the convoy and consequently there was not much chance of survival after being torpedoed. It was pathetic to see little red lights drifting away astern of the convoy knowing with each light was a human life soon to be snuffed out. Standing on the open deck with life jackets on, there was no desire to return to the warmth of one's cabin.

The need for a smoke however was too much for Frank, who went back to his cabin. When he had not returned to the open deck after thirty minutes, Bert decided to go and look for him. He found him sitting on a chair in his cabin, sound asleep, with a cigarette dangling from his mouth oblivious to the depth charges still clanging through the hull. This sleeping in strange positions did not surprise Bert, who had seen him sleep on top of a high wall waiting for the liberty boat to pick him up and take him back to the ship. Once before he had fallen asleep with a cigarette in his mouth and it had burned through the chair and out of the bottom.

On the 23rd September at 4.30 a.m., an American liberty ship called the *Steel Voyager* was torpedoed and sunk. Bert was once again on watch and took the distress call. When finally the attack was deemed to be over, a message was passed round the convoy from the senior officer of the escorts, stating that convoy losses were four ships sunk; two disappeared, feared sunk; one destroyer and one corvette sunk. A very modest total of U-boat casualties was then given stating; one sunk; three probably sunk; two possibly sunk and six severely damaged. This was the biggest defeat that the U-boats had suffered and marked the turning point in the Battle of the North Atlantic. Hitler's main weapon at sea had finally been blunted. No longer would the men of the Merchant Navy feel like "sitting ducks". If the Germans wanted to sink ships then they would have to pay for them with their own lives.

Having survived the worst that U-boats could do, it soon became the turn of nature, and nature came nearer to sinking them than the Germans. They had pumped out all their water ballast and were riding high out of the water ready to sail up the shipping channel into New York harbour. Preparing to take on board the pilot, they received a last minute change of plans. They were to sail unescorted down the coast about 150 miles to the Delaware River and then proceed to a small town called Wilmington, near Philadelphia. The trip would only be overnight but no one had told them about a cyclone. They sailed right into it and had their wits scared out of them. Bert picked up two distress signals from the liberty ships that were breaking up, but the *Thorhild*'s captain, fearing for his own ship without ballast, told Bert that there was nothing that they could do. He confided to Bert that they were in extreme danger of capsizing. His words were prophetic. During the night a huge sea caught them on the beam and over on her side she went. Hanging there she seemed that she did not want to come back. Bert was laying in his bunk and fortunately had tucked the bedclothes round himself, otherwise he would have been thrown to the deck and probably injured. Fully awake he could not move because laying caught up in the bedclothes beside his bunk mattress, it was as if he were held in a straightjacket. Loose objects throughout the ship, such as locker draws and chairs, etc., were flung to starboard as the ship lay over. After what seemed to be an eternity, she started to right herself. In later years Bert was to have nightmares over this incident and never felt happy again when a ship was rolling in a storm. Talking to one of the mates later (he had been on watch at the time), the mate told him that he had thought that the *Thorhild* was going right over. Evidently she had been caught by a large wave and the terrible wind gusts held her over on her side. No doubt it was a miracle that kept them afloat.

Wilmington was a quiet little town compared to New York and

after the past two weeks, was just what the doctor ordered for the crew. Shopping for gifts to take back to England, he walked into a jewellery shop to purchase a signet ring for Hilda. As he walked out of the shop an American couple stopped him and said "They are taking the young men so very young now in England." He did not know whether to be annoyed or friendly, because he no longer felt young. Giving them the benefit of the doubt, he smiled at them and commenced a conversation. Before he knew what was happening he was being taken in tow by them to be entertained. Their friendliness soon "captured" a RN seaman and then of all people, Frank who happened to be looking in the shop windows. Frank was not so sure of being "picked" up like this, but the trio went along out of politeness. What a wonderful afternoon and evening this charming American couple gave them. Eventually in the early hours of the morning, they bedded them down on the lounge room floor, until it was time for them to return to their ships. Before they left, they took their photographs and addresses with a promise that they would write to their mothers. A promise that Bert was happy to find was kept by these wonderful people.

The return trip to the UK was completely the opposite to their outward bound trip; in fact quite enjoyable. It was a bit of a diversion to the humdrum of everyday shipboard life to have the destroyers coming astern of the *Thorhild* to be refuelled. A line would be fired from the destroyer to the *Thorhild* and then the pipe hauled on board. It was for all the world like a mother feeding her young and it gave the escorts a longer time at sea. The dramatic manoeuvre however was when the destroyers came alongside to take on board the depth charges from the *Thorhild*'s fore deck. The two vessels would pitch and roll perilously close together as a depth charge was hoisted across the void between the ships. It was a tricky operation and one that took maximum concentration on everyone's part. The Norwegians were great seamen and the RN so well drilled, they both made it look easy.

Arriving in home waters, the *Thorhild* was ordered to Heysham, just north of Blackpool, and about sixty miles from Liverpool. Bert was allowed twenty-four hours' leave and travelled to Liverpool by train on the Wednesday, returning to the ship on the Thursday night.

The first person to greet him was Frank, who questioned him on his return. Frank was able to inform him that the *Thorhild* was sailing to Birkenhead the next day, so he had wasted his time returning. To say Bert was annoyed was putting it mildly and made plans to leave again by the first train out of Heysham the next morning.

Frank gave him a call as arranged and once again he found himself bound for Liverpool aboard the Irish Mail. This very fast "loco" soon had him in Liverpool where he was to spend two more enjoyable days, not thinking of the consequences if the ship's orders were changed.

On the Saturday morning he decided that he had better travel over to Birkenhead in search of the *Thorhild*. Accompanied by Hilda, they crossed over to Birkenhead by ferry and soon spotted the *Thorhild* from the dock road. As they walked towards her, a local policeman stopped them and told Hilda she could go no further. Bert would have to go on by himself.

Once on board, he was confronted by the chief mate who remembered the incident of his going ashore in Avonmouth. He was not amused and told him that on leaving Heysham a destroyer had called them up by Aldis lamp and they wanted Bert to read the signal. Why him, he did not say, because there were two other sparks on board. He would never have left the ship if it depended on him alone. He never bothered to defend his action because he had been found out, so why make excuses! He was told to stay on board, but refused, telling the mate that his girlfriend was left on the dock road. The mate knew that Bert could have signed off the ship, if he had insisted he stay on board, so grudgingly he said "Very well then, but be back on board in the morning because we will be sailing."

Leaving the ship, he was further aroused when he met Hilda again, who told him that the policeman had done his best to make a date with her. The PC had told her that her boyfriend would be at sea tomorrow, but he would be still there. This left a nasty taste in Bert's mouth regarding men who stayed behind sheltering behind their uniform, while the likes of him were risking their lives to feed them.

The *Thorhild* sailed on the Sunday morning, and Bert decided that this would be his last trip in her. The crew were expecting the *Thorhild* to enter dry dock for one month in New York to have her tanks surveyed and cleaned. This would have been wonderful for Bert, with no shipboard duties. However they were to be disappointed. When they arrived in New York, they started to take on oil again. New York was starting to prepare for Christmas and even the weather had turned cold. The wind did not only blow, it cut through you. Bert decided enough was enough, he would leave the ship in the UK and not bother about waiting for a one month's break in New York. He also worked it out that he could sit for his Second Class Certificate, and in so doing have Christmas at home. He visited the Bronx to say goodbye to Mary and John, not knowing that he would never see them again.

Arriving back in the UK, it seemed only fitting that they should complete their voyage as close to Bert's home as was possible. They were to discharge their oil at the Dingle Oil Terminal only two miles from where he lived. How the memories came flooding back to him of his Home Guard days when he had stood guard and looked out for mines in the Mersey from this very same spot. Once alongside it did not seem that anything could spoil this day. (However, once again he did not bargain on a Merseyside policeman.) He had survived seven and a half months of extreme danger on board a tanker, both from the enemy and the elements. He was to be reunited with his family and girlfriend with a great chance of Christmas at home. Waiting to be cleared by Customs, this PC came aboard and started chatting to him. He wanted to know where Bert lived and on being told just two miles up the road, said "If there is anything that you want to smuggle ashore just put something in here" tapping his hand at the same time. He certainly had picked the wrong person in Bert, because everything he bought overseas he declared. It was not as if he ever brought a lot of goods back, mostly silk stockings with a charge of nine pence on each pair. Annoyed as he was, at the corruption shown by the so-called long arm of the law, he had the last laugh, with this particular "Bobby". Bert had been friendly with a RN gunner on board the *Thorhild*. As was usual the RN sent a van to pick up this gunner and his gear. The gunner asked the van driver if he could possibly give his mate a lift home, which was two miles in the opposite direction. The driver agreed and told Bert to jump in the back which had a canopy over it. At the terminal gates, the PC came out of his office to let the van through the gate. As they drove away there was the very same cop who had wanted bribing to let Bert through the gate with contraband. The look on his face really made up for the anger that had spoilt Bert's first few minutes of docking.

On his arrival home with all his gear, his mother promptly told him to take it through to the laundry, because it was smelling the house of oil. Everything had been washed in readiness for his arrival at home, but he never realised that to landlubbers he was still an oily part of a tanker.

Chapter 8

The *Hardingham*

During the first week in December 1943, Bert returned to the Liverpool Wireless School to prepare for the Second-Class Radio Officer's Certificate. It was day and night cramming, and looking back he cannot believe that he was able to absorb so much technical detail in such a short time. His family and Hilda were very patient with him; they would not distract him during his periods of study.

On the 19th December, he sat his examination in the Liver Building and then waited over the Christmas for the result. To his own, and everyone else's that knew him, joy, his certificate arrived by registered post on the 28th December.

The next day he received a telegram from his soldier father stating "Square Peg now round, I am proud." This more than anything else was the icing on the cake, because his father had always affectionately called him a square peg, because he had not been able to settle down to one job, since leaving school.

In the new year, he decided to join one of the radio companies, instead of signing on at the 'pool'. He applied to the International Marine Radio Company and was accepted. He was sent to a ship belonging to Harrisons of London and called the *Hardingham*. She was berthed in the Eccles Docks, Manchester. Only two years old and of 6,500 tons, she carried general cargo. Her maximum speed was twelve knots.

Signing on this vessel as chief radio officer, he found his quarters on the top deck of the bridge more than comfortable. The crew seemed very friendly, and the officers and engineers, great. Bert's second, was an old hand as regard to war service, but his third sparks was making his first trip to sea. The captain was a friendly Welshman, friendly that is except for an incident on Bert's first day aboard.

He was fastening a photograph of Hilda on his cabin wall by means of a drawing pin, when in stormed the captain. "I will not have objects pinned to the wall on my ship" he stormed. Bert apologised but did not understand his attitude at the time. However a few months later he was to find out the reason and wished he had known at the time of the captain's outburst.

The day after signing on happened to be Hilda's day off and a Saturday at that. He had spoken to her the night before at the hospital and she had agreed to travel to Manchester for the day, so that they could have another day together, before he sailed.

The day was beautiful on Merseyside; clear and frosty. However unknown to Hilda, Manchester was just about suffocated in a blanket of thick smog. Bert left the ship quite early, to meet the Liverpool train in Manchester. He realised on reaching the dock side and looking back, he could hardly see the ship, and that he was in for a difficult time. Feeling his way to the main road, he could not see six feet in front of him. It was more by good fortune that he found the bus stop.

Eventually a bus came alone, and he was amazed to see the conductor walking in front of the bus with a large torch. Boarding the bus he struck up conversation with the passenger sitting next to him, who informed him that he had to be at the station in one hour to catch the London train. He said "I could walk faster than this." To which Bert replied "If I knew where I was, I would be walking." The other passenger said "Come on let's walk, I know the way." It was quite a long walk and it felt as if they would choke, but at least they passed many, many, buses.

Arriving at the station, Bert had the good fortune to be able to just make out the form of Hilda preparing to return to Liverpool. He was one and a half hours late, so Hilda had thought that he could not get away. They went for refreshments and then Bert saw the extent of the filth that he had walked through. His face was covered in black spots, as was his collar and white shirt. Stripping off to his waist, he had to have a good wash down in the restaurant washroom. He dare not think of what was actually on his raincoat, uniform cap and trousers.

During the afternoon, the smog partially cleared, enabling them to look round the city centre, finishing up in a cinema. When the time came for Hilda to board the train to return to Merseyside, he felt very alone and just longed for sailing time to come.

Late Monday morning, they moved from the dock side and commenced their trip down the Manchester Ship Canal. It was a strange experience and did not seem to be real, sailing through countryside, on an oceangoing ship. Bert thought, next week when we are out of sight of land sailing in convoy, this will all seem like a dream. It seemed like a stage production sailing on through villages with its women standing in groups talking while another woman went about her business, pushing her baby in its pram. There were dogs barking up at them, men riding their bicycles alongside them, and cars speeding down country lanes. Only for the fact that they could see their own grey paintwork and nests of oerlikon guns throughout the ship they could have imagined that they were on a holiday cruise. The cows munching away in the fields and the occasional train flashing by in the distance, all added to this feeling of tranquillity. A few weeks from now he would close his eyes and try to conjure up this scene in his memory.

Eventually the locks at Eastham were reached and they could pass out into a more natural environment for an oceangoing ship, the River Mersey. They anchored off Cammel Lairds for the night and then sailed for Faslane in the Gareloch. On arrival at Faslane, Bert was given permission to travel to Edinburgh to visit his father before sailing.

Now that he was chief sparks, he had to attend the pre-sailing conference for chief radio officers, to be brought up-to-date on the latest codes and procedures. This had its reward because he was able to have a last run ashore, before sailing. It was nice to have a "pleasure ride" in the motor lifeboat. The masters had their own conference and on the way back to the *Hardingham* her skipper told Bert the good news — besides having a Woolworth carrier with them, she would be fitted out with "Sea-fires". These were modified Spitfires. There was a great deal of excitement throughout the convoy when these planes were spotted taking off from the carrier. Men who for years had had to take whatever the Germans threw at them, would now finally see the boot on the other foot. Morale was sky-high.

The convoy sailed round Northern Ireland; a great armada of slow, lumbering freighters. As they crossed the Bay of Biscay, seas were as calm as a sheet of glass. The commodore gave orders that all ships fitted with anti-torpedo nets, were to lower them. This was not a popular decision throughout the convoy because it would greatly reduce the speed of the convoy and ships not so fitted naturally resented this slower speed. The *Hardingham* was last ship in her line and was one of the ships fitted with nets. During the lowering of the nets, a cry went up, "man overboard". Evidently a man from another ship ahead of them, had fallen off the net boom. He was swimming strongly and a lifebelt was thrown to him from the *Hardingham*. The *Hardingham*'s captain called Bert onto the bridge and asked him to flash a message to the senior officer of the escort advising him about the seaman in the water. However for reasons unknown, the destroyer either never saw their signal, or chose to ignore it. In sheer frustration the captain turned to Bert and said "I'll make the buggers take notice" and with that gave orders for the *Hardingham* brought right about. No sooner had the ship turned, than this destroyer raced across demanding the reason for such a dangerous manoeuvre. After being given the explanation, the destroyer signalled for them to rejoin the convoy immediately, she would carry on the search for the seaman. Fortunately for the *Hardingham* there had been no lurking U-boats, and after what seemed hours she caught up with the convoy. Later it was learned that the seaman had not been found and every man on the *Hardingham* was visibly distressed. It seemed such a simple accident in ideal conditions. Who could have guessed it would end so tragically? It became more unthinkable when the commodore gave the order to raise the nets and they were never lowered again.

As the light started to fade in the late afternoon, seven Focke Wulf long-range bombers made their appearance in the vicinity of the convoy not knowing that there were Sea-fires waiting for them. One bomber was definitely shot down and the others made off with smoke pouring from them, suggesting that they probably would not make it "home". This was a big thrill for the men of the Merchant Navy and helped to cheer up the men of the *Hardingham*.

The convoy arrived at Gibraltar and the ships sailing along the North African coast were given naval barrage balloons. Arriving during the night in a severe thunderstorm at Algiers, no one on deck had noticed that the balloon had been struck by lightning and had no doubt come down in flames. The Australian third mate thanked the chief mate at breakfast for bringing in the balloon. The mate looked puzzled and told him that he had not done so. Both went aft to investigate and there was the cable hanging over the side in the water.

Over the next eleven months, they were to play their part as a vital supply ship to the British and Allied Armies. They were to carry munitions, tanks, trucks with their drivers; and maintenance crews, oil, telegraph poles; and NAAFI supplies. They looked on Algiers and Bone as if they were their home ports, sailing to such ports as Naples, Sicily, Brindisi, Táranto, Alexandria, Tunisia, Corsica, Ancona, besides the little publicised landing beaches in Southern

France. They were a lucky ship because they had comparative quiet trips, which was very fortunate when they were carrying over 2,000 tons of ammunition.

Life was very cheap in North Africa, especially between the French and Arabs. Bert loved to hear the stories told by the British Army truck drivers about their exploits driving inland. One such story he never forgot, was about a convoy of trucks moving towards the coast, when one of the vehicles ran over an Arab. The convoy stopped and the Arab was found to be dead. Reporting the incident at the next gendarme post a few miles further on, the troops were surprised at the reaction of the officer in charge. He seemed to become very angry and gesticulated wildly with his hands. This puzzled the troops because they knew that the French had little love for the Arabs. Eventually when he had calmed down, the British officer in charge, asked him what they would do with the body. "Body, body," he repeated and then broke into a smile slapping them on the back. He had thought that they had only injured the Arab and that would have involved a lot of red tape for the French authorities. He had been terribly upset wondering why the British troops had not reversed over the Arab to complete the job.

Bert saw four American soldiers in a Jeep hit an Arab on a railway crossing in Algiers. He was spun round before dropping to the ground, no one going to his assistance. Even among themselves they seemed to show no feelings.

Shells were being loaded on board the *Hardingham* for the 8th Army guns in Italy. One of the Arab stevedores fell down the hold. They brought him out on one of the cradles used for lowering the shells into the hold. Placing him on the hot steel deck, a terrific argument broke out, as to who was going to first lunch break. The second mate, a chunky Scot, ploughed into the middle of the argumentative crowd milling about on the deck and shouted at them to get this man off the ship to hospital. It was quite obvious that the poor fellow had a broken back. The group stopped their argument in shocked amazement and one turned shrugging his shoulders said "He die". It was at times like this that Bert was thankful that he had been born British. To read the signs put up by the military in places like Italy was also something that made him feel happy to be British. Signs that read 'Smallpox, Typhus and Venereal Disease are rife in this town', made him cringe when he thought how degrading it must be for the citizens living there.

He met a school mate in Algiers who was serving in the British Army as a transport driver. They spent a very enjoyable evening at a French family's house. Neither could speak French but they had plenty of laughs trying to make themselves understood by sign language. On the way back to the docks they were "shadowed" by a very sinister group of Arabs. However they kept their distance, no doubt because Reg and Bert were sober.

The ship's donkeyman was less fortunate, the next night. He arrived back on board completely naked and as drunk as a Lord. The Arabs had waylaid him and stripped him. Next morning there was a terrible "to-do". The mate was sent for during breakfast because the donkeyman was standing at the top of the gangway wielding an iron bar threatening to split the skull of the first "bloody" Arab that was game to come up the gangway. It took the mate's intervention to pacify the donkeyman, before work could start for the day.

Another incident that could have got out of hand was when some of the crew returning to the ship after drinking the potent French wine decided that they needed transport. Passing the tram sheds, some wag suggested taking a tramcar and driving it back to the docks. The group all walked into the sheds singing merrily and laughing loudly, boarded the first tram. A freshly-awakened group of Arabs came at them with picks and shovels. Evidently these Arabs used the trams as their sleeping quarters. The ship's crew quickly sobered up and took off with the Arabs in hot pursuit.

Bert was surprised to learn that the Arabs in Algeria had plenty of money. Their ragged appearance fooling the visitor into thinking that they were all beggars. It was said that the French would not allow them to purchase their goods, so consequently they had rolls of paper money.

One evening as Bert was leaving the docks, an Arab came up to him and offered to buy his shoes. Thinking that it was a joke, he told the Arab to wait and returned to the ship for his other pair of shoes that needed sole and heeling. Returning to the spot where he had left the Arab, he was surprised to find him still waiting. Handing over the shoes he expected an argument over the state of the sole and was quite surprised when the Arab pulled out a great wad of notes from under his rags and proceeded to peal off, what was agreed upon. Later Bert was able to purchase a new pair of shoes at the officers' shop and had enough money to take a mate for a drink and a cinema show. A few weeks later, when his other pair of shoes required repairing, he took them ashore and had no trouble finding a customer for them and so finished up well shod and entertained with no outlay.

Naples seemed to be always their destination during those first few months. They missed out on the Good Friday eruption of Mount Vesuvius by a few hours having sailed in the morning.

However, they became used to seeing Stromboli, with its ever-flowing lava, running into the sea, in a great cloud of steam. Mount Etna and the Straits of Messina became as familiar to them as any landmarks in the UK. They seemed to be on a monotonous ferry run with no end in sight.

On one of the many trips to Naples, Bert joined a Forces tour of Pompeii. This made a very pleasant and entertaining interlude and learned more in that afternoon about the destruction of Pompeii from the very vocal Italian guide, than he had done from his teachers at school. The guide was a fountain of knowledge and knew every inch of the ruins.

The Palace in Naples was a majestic place overlooking the harbour. It had been taken over by the British NAAFI. Generally the Yanks were first to take over the best places, but somehow this time they had missed out. Nothing was nicer for tired servicemen that to sit under sunshades looking out at the beautiful blue sea and Naples Harbour, while sipping cool drinks. Naples itself seemed a blot on the beautiful Mediterranean. It was rundown, with plenty of beggars troubling the passers-by. The people were very poor and women sat in the main street with their busts out picking fleas from themselves. The scruffy little street urchins were far ahead of their years, sexually. Walking through the Naples streets it was a continuous plea from these children of "Hey mister, you want pretty girl, very clean, very cheap, my sister." Dirty old men also peddled sex with a similar cry (with a slight variation) of "You want pretty girl, very clean, very cheap, my daughter."

The crew of the *Hardingham* had the swimming craze. No matter where they were, no sooner had the anchor dropped than they would be over the side swimming. Bert looks back now and shudders at some of the places where he swam.

One such place was called the deep tank on board the *Hardingham*. They were en route once again from Algiers to Italy. The hatch covers were off the deep tank which was filled with sea water for ballast. The deep tank on board a frieghter is used for carrying liquids. One afternoon Bert thought that it might be a good idea if he used it as a swimming pool. Together with the third sparks, they climbed down into the hold and jumped into the water. Apart for a shaft of sunlight it was quite dark and the water very "rusty". Both thought that they were very clever having a swim aboard a freighter at sea until they climbed back out of the hold. Their skin had turned an orange colour and Bert's underpants were definitely orange instead of white. Needless to say this would be their first and last swim in the tank.

Bone had lovely beaches within walking distance of the docks.

E

One day at lunch it was suggested that a few of the officers form a swimming party after the meal. Bert did not need to be asked twice and joined them. Once at the beach he swam quite some distance out from the shore, enjoying the pleasure of the warm clear water. Swimming back to shore he was quite close in when he was called by the second engineer. Not realising that he was in trouble and thinking that he wanted to tell him something, he swam over towards him. As he was about to ask him what he wanted the second grabbed him in his arms and both went down. Bert felt that his lungs would burst and just when he thought that he could no longer hold his breath he found himself shooting to the surface. Reaching the surface he gulped at the sweet fresh air. He still remembers how good it was to be able to breathe once again. The engineer broke surface behind him and he too was spluttering and coughing. When he had stopped struggling and looked as if he might go down for good, Bert swam round the back of him and putting into practice what he had been taught at school put his life-saving technique to good use. Once in shallow water there were willing hands to take the burden off him. The second was a very big heavy man and Bert a very slim nine stone, four pounds. When he was dragged up the beach it looked as if the engineer was dead. His eyes were rolled right back with only the whites showing. Someone raced up to the road and hailed a private French car. The people in the car took him to the hospital where he eventually recovered. He had been placed on a trestle table with one end sloping to the ground so that his feet were much higher than his head. The sea water that ran out of his mouth was unbelievable and left a great puddle on the floor. His first words on recovering consciousness were "Sister, I want a shit." His much relieved friends realised then, that he was back in the land of the living. He was indeed a lucky man because as a non-swimmer he had wandered into a bomb crater close into the shore.

Later when he was back on board ship, Bert asked him could he remember how he had managed to get away from his grasp. The engineer told him that he had kicked him in the stomach.

When the beach party arrived back to the ship, the captain sent for him and asked him had they been drinking. Indignantly Bert replied, "Definitely not, and for your information I am a non-drinker." This question annoyed Bert for a long time to come especially after such a near tragedy and one that could have cost him his own life.

A lighter side to the swimming pastime happened when they arrived in Naples Bay. The *Hardingham* was carrying trucks with their drivers and a French 'Supply General'. He brought along a pet duck, cared for by his batman. Always ready for a joke, the crew talked the batman into letting the duck go for a swim in the sea, with a long cord tied to one of its legs. The duck was taken over the side by one of the swimmers and placed in the water. Once free, the duck paddled away for its life, until it was at the end of its cord and then it tipped forward like a toy. It was so unexpected that the men lining the rails let out a roar of laughter. Before the general left the ship, a few of the crew hid the duck and told the worried batman how tasty it had been. The poor fellow was nearly demented and told how he had been betrayed by so-called friends and now he would be court martialled. Leaving the ship with the general, he was once again all smiles when the duck was handed back to him, safely in its cage.

Bert was always on duty in the wireless room during action stations. His second and third sparks were posted to oerlikon guns. He longed to squeeze the trigger of a rapid-firing gun just once. A visit to Bone brought about his wish being granted. The RN invited all seamen who had received no instruction on firing weapons to assemble at the end of the mole by 10.30 a.m. — Bert eager for the opportunity was the first there. When others arrived, the gunner gave instructions on how to load and fire a twin "Browning". He then asked for a volunteer and Bert rushed forward. He was told to stand on the box and to watch when firing because the gun only had one magazine loaded and it would have a tendency to swing to one side. Holding his breath as instructed, he looked through the sights and pressed the trigger. As it fired it swung him to one side but he still kept firing even when he fell off the box. A great shoulder, charged at him, knocking him free of the gun. Faces appeared from the back of some of the boulders and then he realised he had scared the daylights out of the whole group who had fled for cover. From that moment on he was cured of wanting to fire a gun.

A very strange experience happened during a thunderstorm as they made their way along the North African coast. No doubt their 2,000 tons of ammunition made it all the more weird and scary. Bert was on his watch 8 p.m. to midnight and owing to the severity of the storm could not keep his headphones on his head. There was a safety device fitted to protect the set from the lightning strikes, but the continuous noise through the headset made it impossible to hear anything. The captain came into the wireless room very excited and told Bert to come and have a look. When Bert went out onto the bridge, he could not believe his eyes. The whole ship seemed to be alive with little blue lights. They were running along the aerials, the rigging, the masts and round the ship's rails. The sight was fantastic, just like something out of a Hitchcock film. When he asked what it was he was told "St Elmos' fire". Normally it only happens round the head of the ship's masts. On this occasion however, the ship must have taken some terrific lightning strikes and been something out of the ordinary to get the usually dour captain excited.

In Alexandria, Bert had a sample of the dexterity of the pickpockets. He was walking away from the GPO in Mohammed Ali Square and had just put away his fountain pen in his uniform top pocket when he was accosted by a young woman carrying a baby. She stopped in front of him saying "You kind officer, please give money." He knew better than to give her money because he would have been plagued by the young children who watched every move of the people in the street. In no uncertain language he told her to get lost and stepped round her. A few paces further on, he felt unconsciously for his pen and found it had gone. It remained a mystery as to how the woman had managed to take it without him seeing her.

A more impressive piece of pocket-picking took place a few minutes later. A tram was crossing the square, crowded as was the usual case. Hanging onto the outside rail was a male passenger with two Arabs running alongside going through his pockets without him suspecting. It was a terrific scene Bert thought for a movie.

Another amusing scene could have been shot a little way further on in Sister Street. This was the red-light street, infamous to seafarers throughout the world. A rather full party of RN ratings were trying to crowd aboard a horse-drawn gharry with its fez-wearing driver gesticulating and swearing loudly. The inevitable happened, through sheer weight of numbers, the vehicle tipped backwards with the horse lifted completely off the ground. Eventually sanity returned and a diminished number of ratings took off up the road. Last seen a street urchin was running away with a rating's cap, having grabbed it from over the back of the gharry.

The *Hardingham* was a very happy ship and the crew really did love their sport. During one of the trips someone suggested having a few rounds of boxing. A ring was prepared over one of the hatches and gloves were produced. Wiggins the Australian third mate and shipboard friend of Bert's, challenged him to a few "rounds". Bert was never keen on boxing and tried to decline the offer; however, Wiggins would not be put off. He called out "You Pommie bastard, are you scared?'' Bert had become used to this "Pommie bastard" which he found to be a term of mateship in Australia to English people, but one thing that he was not going to allow and that was for anyone to think that he was scared. Reluctantly he pulled on the gloves and the fight started. Bert has never been sure whether it was self-preservation or natural instincts born in Liverpool, coming out, but no one was more surprised than he was, when they stopped the fight. The third was bent over, complaining of his nose and the back of his neck.

Later the captain asked Bert where he had learned to fight like that? (He had been watching from up on the bridge.) When he was told that he had never been taught and did not like fighting, the captain replied "That is good, because the way you fight you will kill someone.'' Bert has never been sure whether he was pulling his leg or was serious, but one thing is certain, Bert never pulled on a pair of boxing gloves again.

Wiggins and Bert became closer friends after this incident, so much so they discussed sailing to Australia together after the war. Wiggins' father had been in London at the outbreak of the war and had stayed on. The two had corresponded and discussed buying a yacht and sailing it to Newcastle, Australia, when hostilities ceased. Bert mentioned that he wanted to settle in Australia and would they consider taking him along as a member of the crew. These were pipe dreams, but at least they passed away the hours at sea.

The second sparks, Wiggins, and Bert, spent quite a lot of time ashore, when duties permitted the third mate to leave the ship. Wiggins was a great character behind that dry facade of being an Aussie. He seemed to find a laugh in everything, and enjoyed joking with the local shopkeepers.

One morning the trio thought that they had procured champagne at a bargain price. Returning to the ship with a bottle each they were going to keep it for a "special" occasion. However just before lunch, Wiggins sent for Bert and said "How about sampling my bottle?'' He had the bottle and two glasses ready. Bert reminded him that it was supposed to be for a special occasion; however he told him that he could always go ashore for another bottle if it was anyway decent. They never found out what was in the bottle but it certainly was not champagne. Bert drew the line at two glasses but Wiggins began to acquire a taste for it. In between glasses he persuaded Bert to shave his head because at twenty-three years, he was fast following the family trait of becoming bald, quite young. When the job was complete Bert watched him stand in front of the mirror and feared the worst. The reaction was just the opposite to what he expected. A great grin appreared on his face and he yelled out "You bloody bewdy." His thanks were so profuse that he positively embarrassed Bert, who beat a hasty retreat to the dining saloon for lunch. The captain sat at the head of the table like the father of a family. Bert sat down feeling a little light-headed, but otherwise in full control. Just when the soup had been served, a loud Australian voice from the doorway asked, "How do you feel now Sparks?" Bert very self-consciously turned round and replied "Good" — to which Wiggins said, "Well I feel pissed." Everyone kept their head down and the outbreak was ignored. During the remainder of the meal both kept quiet and no comment was made of the incident by the captain.

The Normandy landings had passed successfully and the news from the battle fronts was good. There appeared assemblies of imitation landing craft at various ports where they called in. Whether they fooled the Germans was anybody's guess. However there were plenty of landing craft sailing quite openly throughout the Mediterranean and it did not take much imagination to feel that another big landing was in the offing. Rumours came thick and fast, but all knew it would not be too long before they would be in the thick of it. The Allies were pressing on up Italy, so no one could say where another landing was likely to take place.

The *Hardingham* arrived in Algiers just in time for Bert's 21st birthday. Unfortunately they were to spend a week at anchor. There were ships of all sizes jamming the port facilities and anchored all round the huge bay. Here then was proof of something big. Bert was fortunate in the fact that he and the second sparks were taken by the ship's boat to the quayside from where they would walk to the RN mail office. This in itself was a nice interlude denied to the rest of the crew.

One incident that reawakened memories of his first meeting with the captain, happened in Algiers. Bert removed the wooden side of his bunk to do his ironing. This made an excellent ironing board when placed from his bunk to his desk, and covered with a blanket. He noticed something crawling along the board. More out of curiosity, he placed the insect in a matchbox and took it to the chief steward. When he asked the chief had he seen anything like what was in the box, he was sickened on being told, "Yes, it is a bug." He returned to his cabin to check if there were more and was horrified to find that the mattress was virtually alive. Returning to the chief steward he was informed that although it was a new ship, the cabin had been "alive" with bugs the previous trip. This then was the reason behind the captain's anger when he had tried to pin Hilda's photograph to the wall. Bert felt betrayed and could not have felt any worse had he contacted the plague. One thing he was sure about and that was he would not share his cabin with any livestock. The chief steward gave him one dozen tins of Keatings Powder and told him to sprinkle it around. At 2 p.m. he locked himself in the cabin and commenced to eradicate the bugs. He stripped everything down, drawers were emptied and even his books he went through a page at a time. To him this was the most revolting and nauseating task that he had ever performed. He checked every inch of his cabin and powdered it until it looked as if a snowstorm had hit it. As he found bugs, he crushed them to make sure they were dead. The smell of the powder and the crushed bugs is one that he will never forget. Finally he stripped off every stitch of clothing and put them in to soak. After vacuuming and rechecking everywhere, he showered and then went out onto the deck for fresh air, feeling too sick for dinner. He insists that this was his worst experience at sea. It gave him a great deal of satisfaction for the remaining months that he was to spend on board the *Hardingham*, he would not see another bug. He would never trust his steward again, because he was responsible for clean sheets and the stripping of his bunk. Every few days Bert himself would carry out a careful inspection.

Eventually the *Hardingham* obtained a berth and started taking on ammunition. Time was fast approaching for that something "big". Late in July, they sailed in convoy for Naples. They had a scare when a German plane flew over the convoy, evidently on reconnaissance. Carrying so much ammunition, made everyone on board apprehensive, although no one would show it. Bert had his own thoughts and wondered if you would know if you were hit. Strangely enough, the closer they sailed to enemy territory the more relaxed they became.

Arriving in Naples Bay, they were shocked to see so many ships. There appeared to be hundreds. Bert had become used to the hundred-plus convoys in the North Atlantic, but had never seen anything like this; it was as if every allied ship afloat was there. The *Hardingham* could not get an anchorage, so she was sent round the headland to a little place called Bagnoli, which was about ten miles by road from Naples.

It was during their stay here that Bert decided to hitchhike into Naples and try to get medical treatment for his stomach. He had been suffering much discomfort and indigestion.

Thumbing a lift by military vehicle, he arrived at a large military hospital, which in happier days had been a school. Entering the hospital he noticed a long queue and presumed that it was for out-patients. He stood there for ten minutes and then decided to find out how long the queue actually was. He found to his amazement that it turned the corner and then along another corridor only to turn another corner and carry on. Eventually he came to the head of the queue where a great notice hung saying "Form queue here for the treatment of Venereal Disease". Bert's legs went weak to think that he had joined this queue.

Walking very quickly he left the hospital without treatment for his stomach. On the way down the corridor he passed an old AB from the *Hardingham* standing in the queue, but pretended not to see him.

Arriving back on board ship he received little sympathy from Wiggins after he had related his experience.

Orders came for them to sail by means of a small convoy to Napoleon's birthplace, Ajaccio in Corsica. It was a most beautiful place and ideal for a holiday. Compared to a lot of other places it was so clean. The swimming was great and there were very fine walks in lovely scenery. Bert wished that they could spend a few weeks here. To think that they were now enjoying what only the very rich could afford in peacetime.

Peace and tranquillity was shattered one morning when the ship's radio announced that American troops had landed in Southern France. Bert found that the exact spot was called San Tropez and the landing took place on the 15th August 1944. This then was why they were so close to the South of France.

In a matter of hours they were sailing towards the French coast and arrived just two days after the actual landing. The landing had turned out to be an anticlimax after the Normandy landings. The *Hardingham*'s crew had expected to sail in towards the beach through heavy shellfire and maybe bombing, but actually sailed in on a sea so serene that it seemed unreal and a quietness that they could not believe. They had built themselves to a state of readiness for the worst and now they could not comprehend the peace. Once the anchorage was secured, off came the hatch covers and out from the beach came the amphibious ducks and barges like a stream of ants. When darkness fell it was an unbelieveable sight. Ships loaded down with ammunition, floodlit with great clusters of deck lights, carrying on the discharge of their highly-explosive cargoes. What a target if Jerry could have reached them. They were told that when the first wave of Americans went ashore, the Germans turned tail and ran. Evidently they were not front-line troops and were made up of a large number of young boys. Mr Churchill had been a spectator at the landing and no doubt had enjoyed every minute of it.

The second night at the beachhead there was one huge scare. The American warships formed a screen along the coast. Cruisers and destroyers searched diligently for U-boats and E-boats that might have tried to get among the supply ships. Without warning, naval guns started to boom out and all the ships switched off their lights. A motor torpedo boat raced out from somewhere inshore laying a thick smoke screen. Bert was keeping an RT watch when suddenly the silence was broken by an American voice calling out "I have a bearing, so-and-so, and I am about to open fire."

The next instant all hell seemed to break loose. To the merchant ships seemingly caught with their pants down, it must be a battleship. The *Hardingham*'s captain raced into the wireless room wanting to know what the bloody hell was going on. The voices coming over the RT were very excited when suddenly a voice boomed out "Snowdrop here, cease fire, you are firing at me." The *Hardingham*'s captain simply said "Well I'll be buggered." The firing ceased and then another voice said "I am going alongside to board." It reminded Bert of the days of Drake. Whoever boarded the enemy ship was told to report immediately of his capture to his senior officer. When the report came through it was greeted with roars of laughter from the captain. Evidently the Yanks had captured a small fishing vessel with three Germans aboard, trying to make a break for it from the Americans. The captain dryly remarked "If those so-and-so Yanks have made us want to change our trousers, what have they done to those poor buggers that they have been firing at for the past twenty minutes?" It really was a comedy for all concerned, when it was realised that there had never been any danger.

This was the only scare that they were to have and it proved to be quite pleasant laying off the beach swimming from off the ship. The water was very beautiful and teeming with fish.

One afternoon, a few of the swimmers decided to try and hitch a lift to the shore. Needless to say Bert was in the group and keen to step ashore in Southern France. They persuaded one of the "duck" drivers to give them a lift ashore. Dangling their feet over the side as they moved in shore, a very large stingray swept by giving them something to think about of what could be in the water.

Once ashore they realised what a beautiful beach it was and apart for a huge mound of discarded life belts and the vehicles making their way in and out of the water; how distant it now seemed from the war.

Tiring of just walking along the sand, they decided to thumb a lift back to the ship. Hailing another "duck", they were just about to enter the water when an American Snowdrop (military policeman) with rifle raised, stopped the "duck" and ordered the swimmers off the vehicle. He asked them where they thought that they were going? And when told "Back to the ship," he told them that they had better start swimming. He was typical of one of the arrogant Americans who got up the noses of British serving men. It was no good remonstrating with him because he held the gun. No one complained because they all had pride and would not let this so-and-so Yank see that he had gained a victory over them.

Every man reached the ship safely, but it took Bert one and a half hours to do so. It was the longest swim that he would ever be called upon to make, but one that he was always proud to remember. He arrived on board twenty minutes late for his watch, but what did that matter, he was the boss, even he never abused this position unless it was an emergency and he considered this to be one, now. One thing that the long swim taught him, was that you can accomplish anything if you try; if he had not been in a desperate situation, he would never have guessed that he could swim so far.

Returning from the beachhead they resumed their ferrying of supplies to the various ports. During one of these trips they carried French colonial troops with their transport. These troops were able to enter the holds on the pretext that they were keeping a check on their vehicles, when in fact they were pilfering field supplies. These K rations contained biscuits, coffee powder, sugar, coffee whitener and three cigarettes. When the time came to discharge the cargo and the hatch covers were removed, there a shocking sight greeted the seamen. Thousands of boxes of rations had been broken open and their contents strewn all over the hold. All this damage to obtain three cigarettes from each pack. With so much food scattered around, the rat population had really multiplied and the *Hardingham* was almost overrun.

One rat entered Bert's cabin when he was reading a book, but was soon put to flight. The third sparks had the terrible experience of finding one on his chest when he woke up, which quickly disappeared when he sat up in panic.

The ship's cat had a great time when they arrived in Taranto and removed the hatch covers for unloading. The cat had had a litter of kittens and really went on the rampage against the rats. The first night it stalked round the ship until it had caught seventeen rats. Some of the rats it would take back alive to its kittens who would then proceed to pounce on it until the mother decided that they had

had enough and then would quickly kill it herself. The second night there was a repeat performance with a tally of eighteen rats, followed by the third night with a tally of fifteen rats. Fortunately for the rats the *Hardingham* sailed before the fourth night. It seemed that the cat was hell bent of ridding the ship of the "plague" herself.

Arriving in Algiers, they received the startling news that a ship had brought the bubonic plague into the port and that all ships had to be fumigated. They tied up and were quickly taken ashore to a very nice small French hotel, while the ship was fumigated. Returning to the ship the next day, it was funny to see rats bloated like soccer balls floating with their tails straight up in the water.

Bert had a most remarkable experience in the Merchant Navy Club in Algiers. He had seated himself at a table for two people waiting for his second sparks to bring over the drinks from the counter. A voice said to him, "Do you mind if I sit here until I have finished my drink?" Looking up he was shocked to see what appeared to be an older face of his schoolboy pal, from Granby Street School. Bert looked at him and then said "Your name wouldn't be Travers, would it?" When told with puzzlement that it was, Bert asked him if he had ever heard of Bert Holden. Mr Travers was shocked because he had heard his son mention Bert's name so often when he was home (which was very little during peacetime) and yet had never met him. Both were astounded at the coincidence, the way their paths had passed and yet they were never to meet again.

It was in Algiers that Bert and the second sparks were taken for dinner to the British Consul's house. They were a charming couple; the wife being French was an excellent cook. Little did Bert know that this would be his last trip ashore with the second sparks because he was to be invalided back to the UK before the ship sailed again.

Trips became boring now, because the chance of enemy action had receded so much. Their escorts became a joke — Italian destroyers with their own crew and one British officer in charge. Wireless watches became a chore of four-on and four-off for Bert and his third sparks through the departure of the second sparks who had returned to the UK. Fortunately the time spent at sea was no longer than five to six days. Summer had given way to Autumn and the crew were getting restless with the backward and forward trips. Rumours flew thick and fast regarding their destination. First it was Bombay after picking up a cargo from Alexandria. Then another rumour, that Wiggins and Bert would not have minded had it been true, and that was they were bound for Alexandria and then to Australia. They did sail to Alexandria but after loading up sailed right back to Italy. A favourite saying on board ship was "Did you hear that on the galley radio?" This would be in response to the latest rumour.

One day in early November, there was the most seemingly outrageous rumour that the crew had heard to date. It seemed so crazy that it was a wonder that it was repeated. The ship was berthed at the foot of Mount Etna in the port of Catánia. As was usual the rumour started "on good authority" and went as follows "The *Hardingham* was to take supplies from Catánia to Ancona in the North of Italy, on the Adriatic coast. They were then to return to Catánia to load up with a cargo of lemons and sail to the UK with them as a Christmas treat to the people in the British Isles." Further to the tale it was reported that the *Hardingham* had been sold.

When Bert was given this news his first reaction was to say "Bull s**t." However when they started to sail up the Adriatic coast, he started wondering and thought 'Well this part is true, dare we hope that the rest could possibly be?'

On the way to Ancona, hundreds of American flying fortresses flew over the convoy at a great height. They were on their way to bomb the "fortress" of Monte Cassino and their noise turned the men's stomachs. Everyone who felt the vibrations of the sound waves, were happy not to be on the receiving end of such a deadly load.

Ancona was reached, with the Germans still fighting grimly for every mile that they forfeited, thirty miles away. It was once again a crazy war with large concentrations of ships being so close to enemy lines. The loss of air supremacy by the Germans, being the key factor. Finally word came through that the rumour that they had heard and scoffed at, was indeed true — they were going home.

New life seemed to be breathed into the crew and it showed on their faces. The weather was clearly showing signs of approaching Winter. A gale sprang up, and out at sea a line of seven water spouts could be clearly seen from the dock area. It was an angry awesome sight.

After unloading, they were taken to moorings to await the first convoy sailing south.

One night, with the wind blowing at gale force, a number of ships, including the *Hardingham* started to break free. Deck crews worked themselves like demons because no one wanted to be marooned in Ancona with damage, especially the *Hardingham*'s crew now that they knew that they were going home. With a head of steam, and one remaining mooring rope, she was saved. Had they been damaged they would have been left to "rot" because there was no ship repairs available in the port.

With much relief they eventually sailed for Catánia. Once at Catánia and they were loading the lemons, they all knew that they were indeed homeward bound. Everything seemed beautiful to Bert, even the four-on and four-off for ten to twelve days of their journey back to the UK. Sailing home with a cargo of lemons seemed to Bert that Christmas had come early. The hatch covers had to be removed at sea when the weather was fine and the lovely citrus smell that filled the ship was most enjoyable.

Sailing up the English Channel without fear of U-boats, E-boats or bombers, was indeed a luxury to them and something only dreamed about a few short months before. Off the Thames Estuary they were puzzled by a strange plane travelling at high speed and with a flame shooting out of its tail. Later they were to find out that they had just witnessed a V1 on its deadly journey to fall on London.

Hull was eventually reached and they docked without incident. The crew were taken to a small office where they signed off the *Hardingham*. It only remained now for the handshakes of a "happy" crew breaking up and that was that. After eleven months together it was like leaving one's family.

Making his way alone to the railway station, Bert did not know that this was the end of his seagoing career. It was the 7th December 1944, and when the strain and tension of the war at sea had been lifted off him for a spell, he realised that he needed a doctor to help him before going back to sea again.

However, it did not quite turn out like this, because the doctor sent him to a military hospital just outside London in Surrey, and after twelve weeks, doctors there decided that he was no longer fit for sea service and he was discharged from the Merchant Navy.

In January 1949, he migrated to Australia with Hilda, whom he had married in 1946. They settled in one of the outer suburbs of Sydney and had one child, a boy, who became a journalist and is now the editor of a local paper. Bert has long since retired from his position as departmental foreman with a leading cigarette company.